***Ultimate Success* has received overwhelming advance praise from a wide audience. Here's a sampling:**

"Profound and insightful, *Ultimate Success* shines a bright light into our busy lives and makes us reevaluate what true success means to us."
Bill McCartney
CEO & founder, PromiseKeepers

"This book is wonderful! Frank not only explains the real truth but also how to personally apply it for a rich and successful life."
Norman Miller
chairman, Interstate Batteries

"This is an incredibly enlightening book and a must for anyone desiring a deeper understanding of what success is all about. The lessons in this book are invaluable, relevant, and potent. This is a book that belongs in your library!"
Jack Williams
president & CEO, Royal Caribbean International

"The author is right on target! In this busy, overstressed world, Frank Beaudine redefines our choices and shows us a road map toward true success."
Tom Landry
former head coach, Dallas Cowboys

"This book does a wonderful job of turning solid concepts into practical understanding and actions. I wish I had read it as a youth."
Ernie Riddle
CEO, Norrell Corp.

"There are many men and women who are chasing the perception of success at the expense of true happiness. Frank Beaudine presents ways to refocus and come back to an equilibrium that includes self, family, and God. This is must reading."
Roy A. Herberger Jr.
president, Thunderbird, The America Graduate School of International Management

"Frank Beaudine's personal stories, examples, and analogies all blend well to portray the heart of his overall message—encouraging those who would seek God's success on his terms."

Dr. Jack W. Hayford
senior pastor, The Church on the Way

"Outstanding! Part 1 is incredibly insightful, and the secrets are phenomenal. Part 2 nails our emotional obstacles; part 3 shows how each of us can have true success now and not in some distant future!"

Wendel Deyo
national director, Athletes in Action

"Frank Beaudine has put together a book that talks about success in godly terms. For those who want to put spiritual values above material values and still succeed in business, this book is a must."

Tony Campolo
speaker, professor, Eastern College

"Who is more successful: Bill Gates or Mother Teresa? If you answered 'Bill Gates,' you need to read Frank Beaudine's book for a better definition of success."

Cal Thomas
syndicated columnist

"This book is a joy to read and shows clearly that the practical and spiritual aspects of our lives must be integrated to live truly successful lives. It will be a help to men and women of all ages."

Oliver J. "Buck" Revell
president, The Revell Group; former FBI executive in charge of all investigations and antiterrorism

"The world says 'do it your way,' but when the top rung is reached, too often our ladder of life is leaning against the wrong building. Seekers of success should find this book enlightening and encouraging."

Brig. Gen. Dick Abel
USAF (ret.); national director, military ministry, Campus Crusade for Christ International

"Spiritual values, appreciation, and recognition of one's life are necessary for us all. In this book, which is not just about success, but about how to achieve happiness, Frank Beaudine gives everyone a road to follow."

Lynn Martin
former secretary of labor, four-time congresswoman from Illinois

"This book is profound in its simplicity and practical approach to the meaning of success. The challenges around success are on the mark regardless of where you are in your career."

Steve Reinemund
chairman & CEO, Frito-Lay, Inc.

"I started to skim this book but couldn't put it down. Then my wife read it, and now we're studying it. The author shows us the way to true success."

John L. Borling
president & CEO, United Way, Chicago; Major General, USAF (ret.)

"It is clear to me that position, power, and money are not giving people peace, joy, and contentment. Frank Beaudine points us back in the right direction. It is great to see that a successful businessman can find the key to successful living."

Dr. John C. Maxwell
founder, Injoy Ministries

"After just reading the introduction, I was ready to endorse this book, but I couldn't stop reading until I finished it. God has used the author to help others see how he wants us to live and how we, too, can enjoy true success."

Craig James
CBS sportscaster & former Pro Bowl back for the New England Patriots

"This is a heartwarming book, filled with real-life examples of men and women who overcame anger, fear, frustration, and despair, whose careers and lives were turned around when they submitted themselves to God's will for them. It is the finest Christian testimony of a businessman that I have ever read."

Dr. G. William Whitehurst
educator, nine-time congressman from Virginia (ret.)

"This book is exceptionally interesting and fulfills the criteria of all good books. It causes you to think, evaluate, and act. Based on Christian principles, it enabled me to find an inner peace that is difficult to find and often more difficult to maintain."

Lou Holtz
CBS sports commentator, former head football coach for the University of Notre Dame

"This is a wise and generous-spirited book. Frank Beaudine, accomplished executive and committed Christian, lets us in on the formula for true success—which, by the way, isn't the same formula the secular world blathers about."

William Murchison
syndicated columnist, author of Reclaiming Morality in America

"The author and I are on the same wavelength. Like him, I discovered long ago that success is using whatever capabililties God gives us to get glory for him. An excellent book."

Dr. D. James Kennedy
senior minister, president & speaker, Coral Ridge Ministries

"This is a book long overdue. Frank Beaudine's wealth of experience as a leader in the executive search industry and his Christian faith have allowed him to author a book that is a real primer for the right way to achieve success."

Richard D. Schultz
executive director, United States Olympic Committee

"This timely book explains how to find real success—that is, happiness, peace, and contentment. It shines a needed light on our success-at-any-price culture and will help the reader avoid the ultimate failure and inevitable personal shipwreck—that of missing life's best by missing life's meaning. A jewel of a book, especially for business and professional people."

Dr. Bill Bright
founder and president, Campus Crusade for Christ

"Frank Beaudine has put the elusive concept of 'success' on a shelf that all can reach. This practical yet biblical approach to the subject will captivate, convict, and correct all who dare to read it."

Dr. Anthony Evans
senior pastor, Oak Cliff Bible Fellowship

"Recognition is not necessarily success! This book is a challenge to rethink your values and to get back on the road to true success."

Dr. Crawford W. Lorritts Jr.
national director, Legacy, Campus Crusade for Christ

"In this book, Frank Beaudine spells out a Bible-based plan for true success in life. It's one that you can start practicing today, whether you're a student or a corporate executive. And it's sure to pay both lifelong and eternal dividends."

Franklin Graham
president, Samaritan's Purse

"Priorities can get out of line from the daily pressures we encounter in a materialistic world. This book will show you the only source for true success."

Dr. David Jeremiah
senior pastor, Shadow Mountain Community Church; president, Christian Heritage College

Ultimate SUCCESS

FRANK R. BEAUDINE

Tyndale House Publishers, Inc.
Wheaton, Illinois

Visit Tyndale's exciting Web site at www.tyndale.com

Published in association with the literary agency of Alive Communications, Inc., 1465 Kelly Johnson Blvd., Suite 320, Colorado Springs, CO 80920.

Designed by Paul Christenson.

Unless otherwise indicated, Scripture quotations are taken from the *New American Standard Bible,* © 1960, 1962, 1963, 1968, 1971, 1972, 1973, 1975, 1977 by The Lockman Foundation. Used by permission.

Scripture quotations marked NIV are taken from the *Holy Bible,* New International Version®. NIV®. Copyright © 1973, 1978, 1984 by International Bible Society. Used by permission of Zondervan Publishing House. All rights reserved.

Scripture quotations marked KJV are taken from the *Holy Bible,* King James Version.

Library of Congress Cataloging-in-Publication Data
Beaudine, Frank R.
    Ultimate success / Frank R. Beaudine.
    p. cm.
  ISBN 0-8423-1721-X (sc)
  1. Success—Religious aspects—Christianity. I. Title.
BV4598.3.B43 1997
248.4—dc21   97-26579

Printed in the United States of America

03 02 01 00
7   6   5   4   3

CONTENTS

FOREWORD

Not long ago, I was traveling to China on a speaking tour, and I used the long plane ride to catch up on my reading and correspondence.

One of the things in my briefcase was a manuscript copy of the book you are now holding. A colleague of mine thought I should read it.

Let me be candid with you: Many manuscripts are thrust into my hands, and while some are excellent, many others are hard to get through. But as I flew across the Pacific that afternoon, I was impressed by the way Frank Beaudine blended the practical and spiritual aspects of our daily lives. His insights on how we can be successful immediately captured my interest. As I kept turning the pages, I began taking notes and jotting down thoughts that I could use for my talks in China.

To clarify and expand on the idea of success, Frank includes real-life stories from his own career and from those with whom he has enjoyed a close relationship. I found these stories particularly captivating and motivational. More than once they tugged at my emotions. The importance and value of having God involved in *all* aspects of our lives comes through loud and clear.

When I returned to the States, I wanted to meet the author.

A friend arranged for me to have lunch with Frank and his son Bob. In meeting Frank, I saw firsthand the love, affection, and respect that he and his son have for each other. During our meal, I learned that Frank and Bob had been working in the same office for the past fifteen years; and for the past seven years, they have served as chairman and president, respectively, of a highly regarded international executive recruitment firm headquartered in Dallas.

Observing their warm father-and-son relationship told me a lot about Frank's character, which played an important part in my participation in this book.

Ultimate Success will help you learn that true success will never be found if you make money the focus of your life. Frank Beaudine has interviewed thousands of men and women of all ages in a broad variety of occupations. He has found that the majority—Christians as well as non-Christians—were focused on faster career growth and increased income and were constantly looking ahead to some future point where they hoped to find financial security, happiness, and contentment. This book will help you see that such a focus is self-limiting and that God has a better plan for success. God's plan will enable you to find the true fruits of success and to make them yours *now,* not sometime in the future.

Regardless of your age, gender, career path, or where you are on the economic ladder, you will find this book helpful. In fact, don't be surprised if you start taking notes or underlining passages just like I did thirty-nine thousand feet above the Pacific Ocean!

Josh McDowell

ACKNOWLEDGMENTS

Many people contributed to the writing of this book, but due to space limitations I am only able to express my thanks and appreciation to those whose help was particularly significant:

To Karen Aune and Wendy Geary,
who gave so freely of their time in the typing
and retyping of the manuscript—
a task that must often have seemed endless.

To Mike Yorkey, the editor of *Focus on the Family*
magazine, for his meaningful editing of the manuscript
in its early stages.

To Greg Johnson, my agent,
who took a chance on me and provided
guidance and support.

To my sons Frank Jr., and Bill, and my daughter Nancy,
who acted as sounding boards as I weaved my way through to
an organized presentation of the material.

To my son Bob, special thanks.
He read all of the drafts and, through constructive
criticism and creative ideas, had a major impact on
the final form the book has taken.

To the folks at Tyndale House who were so supportive and
helpful. Special thanks to Kathy Olson for her outstanding
editing and to Ken Peterson, who devoted so much time
to effectively organizing the material into its final form.

Getting a major publisher turned out to be a problem,
one that on my own I couldn't seem to solve.
I asked God for his help, and he quickly provided the
solution—Josh McDowell. Josh, noted author and leader of
an international Christian ministry, not only agreed to write
a foreword but also, in his typical generous and selfless way,
opened the door for me at Tyndale House.
Despite his own overburdened schedule, he continues to
help and encourage. A special thanks to Josh, a man who
has my respect and admiration. Best of all, he has
become a friend.

Also, special thanks to those outstanding Christian men
and women who have endorsed this book. Their words, as well
as letters in many cases, are appreciated and treasured.

When it comes down to it, though, there is still one person
whose love and support stands out above all others.
Whenever discouragement would rear its head, her love,
confidence, optimism, and faith sustained me—as it always has.
It is to her that I dedicate this book.

To Martha
God's greatest earthly gift to me

Putting Success into Perspective

The first time I met Ray, I was impressed with his intelligence, energy level, and commanding presence. Although he was just in his early thirties, Ray was moving up the management ladder of a large California aircraft-manufacturing company like a rocket. As I got to know him better, I was convinced he had the necessary talent to make it all the way to the top.

Ray and I never became close friends, but because I have a client relationship with his company, we ran into each other fairly often on my trips to southern California. One time, when my wife, Martha, traveled with me to Los Angeles, we made arrangements to have dinner with Ray and his wife, Laurie. We met at a well-known restaurant in Beverly Hills.

We enjoyed a pleasant evening and a wonderful meal, but I was surprised by the amount of alcohol Ray consumed during dinner. Although he became a bit more animated, it didn't seem to affect his speech or his genial mood. When he told us he had recently been promoted to senior vice president, I figured he was just celebrating a bit.

Laurie was a lovely person. She and Ray had one child—a son who was an outstanding football player at a powerhouse university. Tim was a blue-chip athlete, sure to be named All-American that year. Much of our conversation centered around the young man's accomplishments on the gridiron. Ray was excited about the prospect of his son going early in the NFL draft the following spring.

As it turned out, Tim was drafted by the San Diego Chargers in the second round, and Ray called me long-distance to relay the good news. His pride and joy were evident in our conversation. If there was one thing I had learned about Ray over the years, it was that only two subjects really made him sit up and take notice. One was his son's football career. The other was money.

In addition to his management skills, Ray was a shrewd investor with a Midas touch. As he advanced in his company and received generous raises, stock options, and company bonuses, Ray's focus turned to how he could make his money grow. And grow it did: At the time he was promoted to senior vice president, he confided to me that his net worth was already close to $3 million.

Ray was flying high, but little did he know he was heading for a crash. The downward spiral began when the president of Ray's company announced his plans to retire later that year. At the time of the announcement, most people in the company felt that either Ray or the other senior vice president would be elevated into the corner office. Top management insiders believed Ray had the edge.

Between the president's announcement and his actual retirement, however, the pressure began to eat Ray alive. He increased his already heavy work schedule—and his alcohol intake. Two or three martinis with lunch were the norm, and his former relaxed management style changed to a more dictatorial and demanding one. When the president finally retired, few in the company were surprised that the other senior vice president received the nod. When informed of the board's decision, Ray angrily resigned. He couldn't face his colleagues believing that he should be sitting in the president's chair.

I called Ray a few days after his resignation to find out how he was doing. He told me he had already found a new situation—a partner-level position with a New York investment-banking firm. He added that he planned to commute to the East Coast while Laurie sold their house. For a man who had just lost out on a golden opportunity, he seemed very upbeat. I was pleased that he was getting on with his career.

I lost contact with Ray after that, but about six months later I ran into one of his good friends named Ben. He told me the New York job hadn't worked out. Ray had continued his heavy drinking, including liberal use of the readily available cocktails on the first-class coast-to-coast flights. His increasing dependence on alcohol created problems at work and at home.

Ben added that Laurie had moved out of their California home and into an apartment. She told Ray she still loved him, but he had to stop drinking.

The New York firm finally let Ray go, and a week later he voluntarily entered an alcohol treatment program in the Midwest. He was supposed to stay in rehab for a month, but after ten days he walked out and returned to California.

When Ben learned that Ray was back in town, he gave him a call. From the first minute, he could tell Ray was severely depressed. He sounded so morose during their conversation that Ben became alarmed. In a bid to cheer him up, he persuaded Ray to join him for dinner, and they agreed to meet at seven o'clock. But Ray never showed up.

I'll never know what was going through Ray's mind that afternoon and early evening. He was a wealthy man with a beautiful wife who loved him and wanted him back. His son, Tim, had fulfilled all of his dreams and was a highly regarded player in the NFL. Ray had all the material things a man could want.

The police investigation determined that sometime around six o'clock that evening, Ray put the barrel of a gun into his mouth and pulled the trigger. He was forty-five years old.

Failure in "Success"

During most of his career Ray would have been viewed as a successful man by generally accepted standards. His goals were position, power, and money, and he achieved them all.

The peace of mind, happiness, and contentment that he expected from them, however, never materialized, and when the pressures of work built up beyond his control he turned to alcohol for release and became increasingly frustrated, bitter, and unhappy. He saw nowhere to turn, no one to call upon for help, and in that final dark moment took his own life.

I am convinced that there was a solution for Ray and that his life could have been restored. He wouldn't have had to give up the money or the "things" that were so important to him, but he would have had to see them in a different perspective. This book is about that different perspective. It is a perspective that will redefine "success" from the way we're all used to defining it.

Since all of us want to be the very best we can in whatever career path we have chosen, we will also devote attention to how we can make the most of the talents with which each of us has been endowed. If we do that we will find it easier to meet our financial needs and, in many cases, exceed them beyond our expectations. In doing so, however, money must be seen as the result, not the objective. As Ray found out, money is not the key to success.

True success comes from something else, an important life ingredient that Ray, unfortunately, never found.

In Pursuit of Success

Since 1967, I have been an executive recruiter. It is a job that has provided me an opportunity to meet and interview—and even counsel—thousands of men and women from a broad variety of occupations. During our discussions, I have often asked these two questions: "What's your definition of success?" and "Do you think you are leading a successful life?"

Of course, the answers have varied, but in terms of defining success, the majority of them had two common characteristics. The first was the tendency to think of it in terms of the future. They viewed success as being somewhere out in front of them, a sort of destination they hoped to reach someday.

The second characteristic they gave me was simpler: money—and lots of it. Other factors such as level of position, responsibility, authority, and prestige were sometimes mentioned, but unquestionably, money was considered to be the single most important measuring stick.

As we discussed the subject further and they thought about it more deeply, however, it usually became apparent that it wasn't the money itself that represented success to them. Nor was it the things that money could buy. What they really believed was that if they could just get enough money and enough material possessions, they would then have peace of mind, be happy, and be content. It was these fruits of success that they really wanted in their lives, and they thought money was the means to gain them.

In Pursuit of Happiness

The story is told of Benjamin Franklin, who was concluding a moving speech on the guarantees of the Constitution when a heckler shouted, "Aw, those words don't mean anything. Where's all the happiness you say it guarantees us?" Franklin smiled and calmly silenced his critic. "My friend," he said, "the Constitution only guarantees the American people the right to pursue happiness; you have to catch it yourself."

For all the people who are pursuing happiness and success through money, position, and power, there aren't very many people "catching" it.

In 1993, former U.S. Education Secretary William J. Bennett published what he calls his Index of Leading Cultural Indicators. They show that since 1960, "there has been a 560 percent increase in violent crime, more than a 400 percent increase in illegitimate births, a quadrupling in divorce rates, a tripling of the percentage of children living in single-parent homes, and more than a 200 percent increase in teenage suicides."

In my recruiting work I find that many people are unhappy in their jobs, the direction their careers are taking, and the rate of progress they are making. Numerous surveys suggest that high percentages of people don't like their current jobs, don't feel successful, and are living lives filled with frustration, anxiety, and even despair.

An *Industry Week* article (March 4, 1991) indicated that well over 60 percent of those interviewed felt little joy in their workplace. More than seven out of ten men and six out of ten women agreed with the sentiment of one popular bumper sticker: "A bad day at the beach is better than a good day at work."

But some would argue that these things are true only because these people didn't have *enough* money or power to control their lives in the way that would bring them happiness.

I beg to differ.

In October of 1989, the firms of Ernst & Ernst and Yankelovich published a survey of affluent people. Average income of those surveyed was $194,000, and their average net worth was over three-quarters of a million dollars. Although this group represents less than 3 percent of the population, they control more than 30 percent of discretionary income. The results of the survey may surprise a lot of people who are struggling to make ends meet but are hoping someday they too will be at the level of wealth the people surveyed have already reached.

Two-thirds of the respondents said they strongly felt the need to be successful in their jobs, while less than half felt the need to spend more time with their families. Forty percent didn't feel financially secure. A fourth of them didn't feel they had it made, and 20 percent didn't even feel they were financially well off.

While two-thirds felt some guilt about their levels of wealth, only 25 percent gave $2,500 or more to charity each year. Thirty-five percent attended church services regularly, but at the same time, 60 percent felt that in life one sometimes has to compromise one's principles.

Clearly even great wealth and power do not guarantee a happy life.

Likewise, in my recruiting endeavors, the same people I have asked to define success have not been able to say that they were truly successful. Some were satisfied with the progress they were making, but most didn't feel financially secure. They said they had seen their income increase each year, but their cost of living seemed to rise at the same rate. Many expressed apprehension about their future, what with so many companies being acquired, merging, or "downsizing" in today's competitive economy. The possibility of losing their position disrupted their peace of mind. Happiness was sporadic in their lives and easily lost. Contentment was more a concept than a reality.

You see, while people believe that money, financial security, and peace of mind are interrelated, the reality is that these elements have an uneasy and undependable relationship. Even when people have money well in excess of their needs, they discover that by itself, it doesn't guarantee peace of mind.

On a recent trip to Chicago, I had dinner with a business friend and his wife. By any worldly standard, this couple would be considered successful. They owned a downtown condominium at a fashionable address, a large home in the suburbs, plus a vacation home in Florida. The man was president of a manufacturing company, and from previous conversations, I would estimate his net worth in the $7 to $8 million range.

That evening, however, I couldn't get either of them off of

the subject of money. They expressed their concerns about the economy, their investments, and the high taxes they had to pay. I tried, in a low-key way, to let them see how really well off they were and that most of their concerns were based on negative imaginations that were inhibiting the enjoyment of the life with which God had blessed them.

I might as well have been talking to a brick wall. They wouldn't listen. This couple, in their late fifties, began the litany all over: their concerns about the business outlook, how some of their investments were turning sour—and those taxes!

I tried a different tack: pointing out that their financial situation was secure enough that they could even retire. "If you sell your condominium, you can split your time between Chicago and Florida," I noted. "I'm sure you can maintain your current standard of living just from the interest on your investments."

The couple immediately protested. "You don't know how much we have tied up in company stock," the man informed me, adding that the price had dropped 10 percent the past year.

No matter what I said, it was clear that they relied heavily on money for their security, and that their focus was on getting more. Mentally, I shook my head. *To be so rich and to have so little peace of mind.*

In Pursuit of Contentment

For most people, contentment is even more elusive than happiness and peace of mind. The materialistic perspective on contentment is summed up fairly well in the Frank Sinatra song "My Way." In that song, a man is looking back on his life and, while he has some regrets, he has apparently achieved some goals that have provided him with a great deal of satisfaction. He is particularly proud of the fact that he lived his life his way, relying totally on himself, and he seems quite content with the results. It's just a song, of course; in real life contentment is not that easily attained.

In the early years of their careers, people are striving to meet their needs and to get a bit ahead. Expenses tend to increase as they get married and have children, and most people can't put much away during those years. As a result, the striving continues, and contentment is more of a future hope than a present reality.

As people reach middle age and beyond, many will look back on their early goals that were never attained, opportunities that were missed, perhaps the breakup of a marriage, and possibly even estrangement from children. Since the majority of people don't ever amass a lot of money, they may still be struggling with day-to-day financial problems. Very easily a nagging feeling that they missed the boat somewhere along the line can develop, and true contentment seems hard to find.

People who do earn good incomes can also have difficulty with contentment, as we have already shown that material possessions and even luxuries bring only limited satisfaction. Having a lot of "things" tends to breed a desire for more "things." There is always a more expensive car, a larger house, or a vacation home on the lake that has an allure. Even the very wealthy continue to pursue ever greater wealth. They may comment that at their level, the money they accumulate only represents "scorekeeping," but it doesn't seem to dampen their drive to score as high as possible.

Despite their wealth, my friend and his wife in Chicago are not really content with their life or with what they have. The pursuit of more money has shifted their focus away from enjoying life on a day-to-day basis.

Materialism and Christianity

As a Christian, it's easy for me to think that those of us who claim the reality of Jesus Christ in our lives are immune to this emphasis on money as a means to achieving success and happiness. Unfortunately, I have found this simply isn't true.

Probably two-thirds of the people I have interviewed have professed to be Christians, but their definition of success and the anxieties they expressed for the most part matched those of non-Christians. In many of those discussions with Christians, I have posed this question near the end: "How do you view success from a spiritual point of view?"

Invariably my question startles them. I can almost see the mental shifting of gears as they grope to find the "right" response.

Their answers tell me that many Christians are compartmentalizing their lives. They have their work time, their family time, their social time, their civic time, and then—in a compartment marked "Sunday morning"—their God time. They view the secular and spiritual aspects of their lives as separate entities rather than as fully integrated parts of a whole. When it comes to the earning of their daily bread, they approach it from a materialistic perspective rather than from the Christian outlook they otherwise profess to adhere to.

Billy Graham, who has personally known many U.S. presidents and other world leaders throughout his career, refers to this tendency in his book *Just As I Am*. He writes, "Many leaders, I am afraid, place their religious and moral convictions in separate compartments and do not think of the implications of their faith on their responsibilities."

Many of us who are Christians find ourselves in this materialistic trap—we plod on year after year, worrying about making ends meet and trying to stay one step ahead, hoping for the "break" financially that will help us leapfrog toward the "success" that we hope will provide us with the happiness, contentment, and peace of mind we really want.

Why are so many Christians buying into the materialistic perspective? Why would we use that perspective to find limited forms of happiness, contentment, and peace of mind when so much more is available to us?

One reason is that we don't fully understand the biblical perspective. As a result, we are deceived into believing that the pursuit of money is the best way to find the fruits of success. It seems the most practical thing to do.

There is no question, of course, that money is one of life's important realities. In and of itself, there is nothing wrong with it. The coin of the realm is our primary means of exchange for goods and services. Money provides for our family's needs, as well as for luxuries and services that make life more enjoyable.

We must be aware, however, of two basic truths about money. First, money itself and the things it can buy are able to provide only a limited degree of happiness. Regardless of their perspective on success, most people recognize that personal relationships are the source of deeper and more sustainable happiness. A new house, a new car, or other luxuries will provide little happiness if we have no one to share them with.

As Christians we must recognize a second truth as well: Having an excess of money carries with it a responsibility and an accountability for how we use it. If we earn in excess of our needs, we can also do much good with it—such as helping others in need, supporting ministries, and donating to worthwhile charities. Scripture is very clear about our responsibilities if we have been blessed with an excess of material wealth.

The idea of accumulating more and more money has such an allure, however, that it can gradually become our number one priority. If we let that happen, we are keeping God out of a major segment of our lives.

Most Christians don't realize that if making money becomes our most important objective, we are creating a "false god" and placing it in front of the one true God. We have turned our focus back to ourselves, thinking in terms of *our* money, *our* possessions, and *our* accomplishments. When we think this way, even as Christians, the true fruits of success will elude us. In addition, our lives will not flourish as God intends for them to.

Another reason many Christians shift back to a materialistic perspective is due to the cares of the world. Everyone comes up against adversities, trouble, and worries from time to time, but instead of turning to God for guidance and help, we rely on ourselves.

The results are generally disappointing. We are distracted by the circumstances and often don't see a solution to our problems. We either don't know, don't understand, or can't bring ourselves to believe that we have a God who hears our prayers and is fully capable of meeting our needs. While we will readily agree that God is interested in the spiritual aspects of our lives, we have difficulty understanding that he cares about the practical aspects as well.

True Success

The path to true success begins with reevaluating what success means. True success is not achieving what others consider important, nor is it accumulating money and wealth, nor is it attaining a position of significance and power. True success is found only in becoming what God created us to be.

Early in my career, I became aware that the world operates within a framework of laws and principles. As I read Scripture, however, I realized that these laws and principles are actually manifestations of God's spiritual laws and principles. Established by God, they are always in effect and are unchangeable.

Based on my experience, as well as that of countless others whose careers I have followed, there is a clear correlation between the understanding and use of these principles and the results achieved. When we operate in line with God's principles, our talents are enhanced and we move ahead with relative ease. If we work apart from them, we will find ourselves in a struggle that will limit our progress and even tie our lives up in knots.

In the chapters ahead, we will learn exactly how some of God's laws and principles operate. We will examine some of the steps we can take to enhance the use of our talents. As we do this, we can more easily overcome the cares of the world. We will also look at six of the primary obstacles to effective talent utilization that prevent us from realizing our full potential. And finally, we will consider the path to *Ultimate Success.*

1
Secrets of
SUCCESS

SECRET # 1
Live in the Now,
Not the Later

Roger has risen rapidly in the business world. He is currently one of the youngest division managers at a major diversified company. His prospects are excellent for becoming group vice president. But Roger is a man in a hurry, and he thinks constantly about his next step up the ladder. He worries about other division managers overshadowing his performance, frets over each crisis arising in the plant, and is frequently impatient with his staff. Roger's health is not good; he suffers from headaches and stomach problems. For all his success, he isn't enjoying his life.

Roger is living in the future, worrying about what might happen, nervous about a lot of things he can't control.

Ed is a supervisor in an industrial plant. When he made the move from a union employee over to the management side, he was thrilled with the broader responsibilities and larger income. He and his wife raised their standard of living as Ed looked forward to continuing advancement. However, Ed learned a bit too late that seniority also plays a role in management—it will be some time before he can qualify for a foreman position. Now Ed works overtime to pick up some extra income, and his wife has gone back to work to help pay for their recent spending spree. Ed worries that maybe future advancement won't come fast enough to help them afford the lifestyle to which they've already become accustomed.

Ed has put himself in a position where he has to depend on an unknown future in order to pay for his life in the present.

Roger and Ed reflect the strong tendency of many of us to equate career success with personal success. Higher status, greater influence, and increased income are seen as the things that give us our identity as successful individuals. And so we grab for what we can in our work life.

Indeed, there's a sense of exhilaration and satisfaction when one's capabilities and dedication are recognized and rewarded by senior management. It's natural to want to achieve more, to climb the ladder, to get promoted. Yet business literature is littered with stories like these, lives of dissatisfaction and frustration.

The big problem here, of course, is that in order to attain success for ourselves now, we mortgage our future.

When people ask me for career advice, I tell them that the first step is to maintain a "now" focus in their lives. The past is gone, and we can't relive it. All we have is today. The future lies ahead, but life does not guarantee that it will become a reality.

We need to focus on the "now," not the "later."

The only time we can actually do anything is *now,* yet for a number of reasons, many of us easily lose this focus. We let it shift from where we are and what we are doing to where we *think* we are going and what we *hope* to achieve. In fact, we can concentrate so intently on the future that we live there more than we do in the present.

Someone once said, "If there is hope in the future, there is power in the present." Understanding this principle is vital if we are to reach our full potential.

How can we develop more of a present-focus? I think there are three simple ways:

- Don't let the past cloud your future and ruin your present.
- Don't neglect your current responsibilities.
- Don't pursue goals that no longer make sense for you.

Don't Let the Past Cloud Your Future and Ruin Your Present

William always wanted to be president of his company. Actually, he did have an exciting career with steady growth and responsibility in a major international firm. At forty-five, he was group vice president, and at fifty-five, he was promoted to the firm's number two slot: executive vice president. Five years later, however, he was passed over as chief executive.

Now, every time someone else is promoted within the company, William perceives it as a slap in his face. Because of a situation in his past, he is frustrated about his future. At the age of sixty-two, he is a bitter man.

William will carry out his responsibilities until retirement, but he has shown no enthusiasm for sharing his wealth of experience with younger executives. He thinks back a lot, recalling past achievements, but even his wife is weary of hearing about them.

Don't Neglect Your Current Responsibilities

Sometimes we work so hard at achieving our future success that we neglect our present responsibilities. Sometimes that neglect turns around and sabotages our future plans.

When Tom was named regional sales manager, he immediately started thinking about his next target—general sales manager. From there he would be a shoo-in for vice president, he thought, perhaps with an even larger company. To move his career along, Tom spent a lot of time at headquarters cultivating connections with the "right people." He wrote insightful reports about what new products competitors were introducing, recommended improvements that should be made in the company's product line, and offered incentive ideas for sales growth.

However, it would have been better if Tom had minded his own store. He never solved the recurring distribution problems in his region. Eventually the problems became intolerable to the company. Tom was ultimately reassigned.

While Tom was working on his "later," his "now" was falling apart.

Don't Pursue Goals That No Longer Make Sense for You

As executive vice president, John needed only one more step to realize his longtime goal of running a company. When the president retired, however, the board of directors decided to bring in an outsider.

Passed over, John started looking around and a few months later seized an opportunity to head a smaller company. To others who knew John's abilities and style, the new position didn't make good sense, but John was pursuing a goal he had established for himself, a goal he had determined he just must achieve.

Almost immediately, he encountered a mounting series of problems. Some he had never dealt with before. Both sales and profits started declining, and before a year went by an unsympathetic board turned up the pressure on him to get the company back on track. There was an "or else" implication in their remarks.

John's reaction was predictable. He threw himself into his work with vengeance. He worked longer hours and became more demanding and critical of his staff. The results were also predictable.

Morale at the top management level began to drop, and it wasn't long before the disarray at the top spread throughout the company.

Six months later, John sat at his desk at eight o'clock in the evening staring at the latest P&L statement. As he analyzed the disappointing results, a sense of depression engulfed him.

He dreaded the board of directors meeting that was scheduled for the next morning. As he sat there, he thought about the exhausting work schedule he had been following week after week and how he had been ignoring his family. As he brooded, he finally faced up to the fact that he didn't really like the responsibilities of running a company. He had pursued a goal that didn't make sense for him or for his skills and talents.

He still had almost two years left on his contract, but he was confident the board would work out a mutually agreeable settlement with him. It was with a sense of relief that he took out some paper from his desk drawer and began writing his letter of resignation.

Goals can be good tools for achieving in life—we'll talk about them in the next chapter. But goals that don't match up with who we are or with what we should strive to be can lead us in the wrong direction.

Just like William, Tom, and John, many people today are victims of their own plans for success. They are sabotaged by the past, or neglect the present, or focus so intently on the far-off future that present-day success and satisfaction are closed off to them.

Success Is a Process, Not a Destination

The first secret of success is to live in the present—not in some hedonistic sense, but by simply being aware of the opportunities, joys, and satisfactions of each day. Success is a process, not a destination. As we move along in life, our knowledge and skills increase with experience. This allows us to advance in terms of responsibilities and income. But "now" is the most important reality of life. It is only "now" that we can enjoy the fruits of success. If we are using our talents to the best of our ability and have our priorities—both practical and spiritual—in order, we are successful at this point in time. If we view success as a continuing process rather than as a point in the future, we can be successful at each step along our career path.

We've all seen the overly dedicated type—the workaholic—who sacrifices his family and social activities to attain what he considers to be success. He works long hours, travels frequently, and even brings home work on the weekend. Oddly enough, if you stopped him to ask why he was doing all of this, he would probably say something to the effect that it was for his wife and children. He would also refer to the material things and financial security he is providing his family—the very family he is ignoring in the process.

Then one day he steps out of the future and back into reality only to find that his children are grown and his wife has developed her own set of interests. Even then, he may not realize that he had been living with his attention primarily focused on the future and that he had missed the flavor and pleasure of each today along the way. All too often, this is an underlying cause of marriages falling apart after fifteen, twenty, or even thirty years. Each of the partners was walking a separate path toward some future destination instead of walking hand in hand, each day, along the way.

The Joy of Barbecuing

Recently, during a family barbecue, I was reminded of the principle of living in the now. I got to thinking about other barbecues we'd had as a family.

My experience with barbecuing began shortly after Martha and I purchased our first home many years ago. I was soon hooked on outdoor cooking, finding great pleasure in experimenting with different ways to prepare various meats and trying different recipes for the sauces with which to coat them. Hamburgers, hot dogs, ribs, and chicken just seem to taste better when grilled on a barbecue, and during the warm days of summer that followed, preparing the meat outdoors became a weekend ritual that our growing family enjoyed immensely.

That first home would have to be described as modest at best. It was a prefab set on a thirty-by-forty-foot concrete slab and was almost identical to the hundreds of other homes comprising the particular development where it was located. There were three bedrooms, one bath, a living room, a kitchen with a breakfast nook, and a utility room where the furnace was located. There was no dining room or garage.

The backyard was also small, but it featured a large oak tree under which we had placed a wooden picnic table with benches on each side. There was also a white picket fence that I constructed myself. Putting it up wasn't too bad, but painting all those pickets every other year was a chore.

By today's standards, my first barbecue unit would have to be rated as almost ludicrous. Basically, it consisted of a two-foot aluminum pan shaped like half of a barrel to hold the charcoal briquettes. This was supported by four flimsy aluminum legs. Even when I would embed them an inch or two into the ground, the whole unit still tended to wobble.

To start everything going, I had to remove the grilling surface, put in the charcoal briquettes, douse them with starter fluid, and toss in a match. Usually the fire went out a couple of times before the briquettes caught on, and I would have to spray on more fluid. This was a procedure Martha refused to watch, convinced that the resulting flare-up of flames would sometime burn my hands, arms, and possibly my face. It never did, but I must admit there were some close calls.

As I think back to those years of the past, a particular Saturday afternoon comes to mind—one that was fairly typical.

We had an inflatable plastic wading pool in the yard, and on this particular day my brother, Milt, who was attending college in our city, was spending the day with us. He was cooling off in the wading pool while our two sons and daughter, ranging in ages from two to seven, were alternately playing with him in the pool and running under the water sprinkler we had turned on nearby.

As I started the hamburgers and hot dogs, Martha was in the kitchen putting the finishing touches on the potato salad and the corn on the cob. As the food cooked, the sounds of children's happy laughter filled the air. We ate at the picnic table and, as we first held hands and thanked God for the food and all of his blessings, a great sense of happiness swept over me.

There have been four homes in three different cities throughout the country between that first one and our current home. Each one has been larger, reflecting the need for more room as our family grew and the increased income that comes with career growth.

Our present home is a custom-built ranch style with an attractive swimming pool and Jacuzzi. There are large trees on the property, including ten crepe myrtles that bloom all summer. Hedges and flowering bushes flourish along the sides of the pool, and the patio has a number of lounge chairs and two umbrella-covered tables.

My barbecue is now state of the art. As the teenagers of today might say, it is awesome. It is sturdy, with a cast-iron grilling unit and has a lid and rotisserie. There are actually two grilling surfaces that are suspended over permanent gas-fired coals, and there are two automatic lighters to get the fire started. I can grill directly over the coals or, if I want to cook a roast, I can use the rotisserie or just fire up one side, placing wood chips in a metal container on the coals, with the meat on the other side. The lid closes tightly to form an enclosed oven that has a temperature indicator and control. Handsome wood surfaces run in front and on each side of the unit for carving and to hold foods or condiments. There is also a place to hang the long-handled utensils used in the cooking process.

This past weekend, our daughter, Nancy, our youngest son, Bob, and their families were over for swimming and the inevitable barbecue. Nan and Bob each have three children—four girls and two boys altogether, ranging in age from five to twelve.

As I started to prepare the food, Bob and our son-in-law, Loran, were playing in the pool with the children. Martha, Nan, and Bob's wife, Cheryl, were in the kitchen putting the finishing touches on the salads and the corn on the cob. The sounds of children's happy laughter filled the air. As we all held hands before eating to thank God for the food and his blessings, a great sense of happiness swept over me. I thought back to that afternoon of "then" so many years ago and considered the differences between the two occasions.

We are older, of course, and now it's our children's children who are playing in the water. Our present home is much larger and more lavish than that first one, and the backyard is also larger, with much improved landscaping. A swimming pool has replaced that wading pool of the past, and there is a world of difference between the barbecue units of "now" and "then."

Aside from the fact that we are older, however, all of the differences were material in nature. As I thought about them, I also realized there was one constant. And that constant was the happiness that was present in both situations. What was even more significant was the realization that our happiness was not related to the material changes that had taken place over the years.

We were just as happy then as we are now. We were thrilled with our first home, and we didn't think in terms of what we didn't have. Our children were as happy in their wading pool as our grandchildren are in a swimming pool now. Our happiness was not in any way dependent upon our dreams or hopes for what the future might hold.

True happiness can never be measured simply in material

terms. If we pin our hopes simply on money and what it can buy, we are heading for disappointment and heartache.

It is only natural that as we move along in life, advance in our careers, and have increased income, that we will want to improve our standard of living. There is nothing wrong with having a nice home or car, and there are a variety of other things that make life more interesting and provide forms of pleasure and comfort. But things are just that—things. What we want to grasp and understand is that we were created for higher purposes than just "things."

The mistake many people make is to assume that future affluence will ensure future happiness. That usually isn't true.

Happiness doesn't come from getting a bigger barbecue.

Stop and Smell the Roses

The most satisfied business people, or people in any other endeavor, are those who concentrate on each day as it comes. They are careful not to get locked into a course of action aimed at attaining goals set long ago. Most important, they enjoy the "now" in their lives and understand it's the only time that really counts. Such people have the least difficulty leading full lives in their retirement years.

Some years ago, I played golf with an elderly gentleman who could not hit the ball very far. A triple-bogey was a good hole for him. When he casually mentioned that he used to play scratch golf, I asked why it didn't bother him to score so high.

"I'm just happy to be out here in the sun with nice people, seeing the trees and beautiful flowers," he replied with a warm smile. I could see he meant those sentiments. Then he looked at me and frowned. "You haven't been seeing the flowers, have you?" he asked.

That man taught me more about being a successful golfer than all the lessons I've had from PGA pros. He was right: I hadn't been aware of my surroundings at all—the close-cropped greens, the flower-lined fairways, and the beautiful over-water par 3s.

That's a great lesson that can be applied to life. My golf score isn't any better these days, but each game is more enjoyable because I appreciate the course, the friends, and the game itself. I've learned that there is far more to golf than just the score, just as there is more to life than just work.

Define Your Goals

While we have established the importance of living in the "now," part of that present-focus actually involves setting goals for the future. Having goals for the future helps motivate us to keep taking steps in the right direction—whether it's climbing the corporate ladder or building a relationship with a friend or spouse. Even though goals by their very nature point us toward the future, their greatest value lies in helping us with the day-to-day process of growth.

The importance of setting goals may seem fairly obvious, but many people never do it very effectively—and a surprising number never set goals at all.

Many of us let others set goals for us. From our earliest days of childhood, we are trained to pursue goals set by others. Parents begin that training when they give us various chores, like cleaning our rooms and putting away our toys, that must be completed before we can go out and play. School is the next step. Teachers begin to direct activities, teach the three Rs, and hand out the homework. Doing well on tests and being promoted are goals set for us as we move through grammar school and high school.

During our school days, of course, we have opportunities to set some of our own goals. We can try to excel in our favorite sports, earn high grades, join campus clubs, or run for class president. In these early years, some people start to separate from directed activities and start setting their own goals, but many others drift along without a rudder.

If we go to college, it might stem from our own ambition, but for many, it is just another step along a directed path. Then it's time for a job, marriage, children, and a home. For some, there is self-direction in all of this, but for many others it is more a "doing what is expected" sort of thing, and unfortunately, life can settle into a pattern that is not always fulfilling and, in many cases, vaguely discomforting.

Many of us plod through life like this and never really use the talents God has given us. We do the expected things and perform the responsibilities of work, marriage, and bringing up a family, but we find ourselves just drifting along, sensing that something is missing. We never quite see how we can take control of our lives and make the changes that deep down we would really like to make—changes that will bring more meaning and fulfillment to our lives.

Dreams or Desires

The key to making life changes and to taking more control over our lives lies in learning how to effectively set goals and take steps to achieve them.

Goal-setting has to be considered in terms of attainment. This is, in fact, what actually distinguishes goals from dreams or desires. Goals are concrete, specific, and measurable. As they are achieved, we set new ones, broader ones, higher ones. We build one upon another in a continuing growth pattern as we get to know our talents better and expand our scope in using and applying them.

When Ray Kroc opened his first McDonald's restaurant in 1955, he never could have envisioned thousands of McDonald's restaurants popping up around the world. No, Kroc had a simpler goal back then—making his first restaurant successful and profitable. When that happened, he saw the great potential in serving the American public quick and inexpensive food, and he started opening additional restaurants.

Somewhere along the line, he saw the advantages in franchising McDonald's, which allowed for even more rapid expansion. It then became necessary to establish quality controls, to take advantage of increased purchasing power, to train new employees in uniform procedures, to establish management training (at Hamburger University!), and to come up with new products.

Ray Kroc, along with countless other entrepreneurs, started with a specific goal. When it was achieved, he built and expanded upon it, although he could not possibly have foreseen a McDonald's in every town and hamlet when he set that first goal.

In a similar manner, we cannot foresee where our talents will take us, but we have to start out with a goal.

I think that there are four keys to setting good life goals:

1. A goal should be realistic. That is, we should believe we have the ability or talent to achieve it. Furthermore, even as we set a goal, we should immediately be thinking about attaining it. The key is commitment; we cannot achieve a goal without being committed to its attainment. Understanding what is meant by commitment is vital.

2. Commitment to a goal requires being willing to pay a price. Our willingness to pay the price is related to our base of values at the time we set the goal. This is an important point, because as we go through life our value base will change. That means our willingness to pay a particular price for a particular goal may also change as well.

3. Commitment to a goal requires being unified to achieve a specific objective. We have to decide that we have a specific goal and then believe in our hearts that we can and will achieve it. Finally, what we say—the words that we utter about it—must reflect that decision and belief. We must speak positively, bringing our thoughts, beliefs, and words into line in a positive, undoubting way.

4. *Commitment to a goal requires being persistent.* Various obstacles or adversities will always appear somewhere along the road to goal achievement. If we are easily discouraged, our unity of purpose can be disrupted, our willingness to pay the price may be undermined, and we can let the goal disappear from view.

Let's take a simple situation to help us illustrate these points.

Assume you are sitting in your living room with your spouse. You suddenly realize that you're thirsty. You decide to get a drink of water. At that moment you have set a goal. That decision has set into motion a number of the principles.

First of all, the goal is *realistic:* You know where to go and how to get a drink of water, and you are totally confident that you have the ability to do it. This is not just an abstract idea but something you actually believe you can accomplish without question.

You start by getting up from your chair. Here, another principle is involved. Before making the decision to get a drink of water, you already knew there would be *a price to pay.* You knew you would have to get up out of your easy chair, walk to the kitchen, open the cupboard, get a glass, turn on the faucet, fill the glass, and drink the water. The decision to do all that took only a split second, but the principle remains the same: Any goal involves a price to be paid. In this instance, you are thirsty, so you quickly decide it's worth it.

As you get up, your spouse asks where you are going, and you inform him or her that you're going to get a glass of water. At that moment, you are completely *unified*—in heart, mind, and words—to achieve your goal.

As you enter the kitchen, however, you discover that all the water glasses are dirty and in the dishwasher. Again, a split-second decision takes place. The price to achieve your goal has just gone up as an unexpected obstacle has appeared. You reevaluate and check the magnitude of the new price to be paid. You assess it against your base of values. You decide that you are still mighty thirsty, so you make the decision to press onward—*persistence*. You pull a glass out of the dishwasher, wash it, dry it with a hand towel, and fill it with cool tap water. You take a long sip and quench your thirst. Mission accomplished.

The Problem of Goals That Are Too Ambitious

Of course the glass of water is an extremely simple example. Let's consider something more complex.

Let's say a young man has just graduated from college with a degree in business. Mike lands his first job—an entry-level position—with a shipping company. At the age of twenty-three, Mike decides that his goal is to become president of the company. Now that may be a good long-term direction, but it is not a very good goal. It is virtually impossible for Mike to understand this early in his career what it takes to become president. He can hardly imagine the amount of discipline, management skills, intelligence, social requirements, and ability that are needed to land the corner office. Besides, Mike doesn't know if he would even like the position if he were to attain it one day.

Equally important, when a goal is set too far out, it is very difficult to determine what price will have to be paid in order to achieve it. Considering our young man again, Mike has no clue about the additional training, extra hours, long business travel, and other sacrifices that will be required. All these elements are vague and generally unknown to him at the outset of his career. While his current base of values may convince him that he would do "anything" to become president, the reality is that as he matures, gains experience, and—hopefully—wisdom, his base of values and priorities will change significantly.

In his early years on the job, for example, Mike might be required to travel a great deal. He willingly runs from airport to airport because he believes the experience is vital to his career. Then one day, he meets a young woman, falls in love, and gets married. Suddenly, Mike finds that his base of values has changed. He no longer enjoys three- or four-day stretches away from home. Instead, he wants to spend more time with his wife, Nicole.

Then Amanda is born, and again Mike's value base changes. Any overnight travel seems excessive, and his desire to spend even more time at home with Nicole and Amanda may lead him to reconsider the direction his career is taking. He may even decide to change his career path.

We can't leave out what Nicole is feeling. Before meeting Mike, she had a well-defined career in mind, with well-defined goals. When she married, however, her base of values also changed—and changed again when Amanda was born. Perhaps, after a season of motherhood, she will return to her business career. On the other hand, she may feel completely content in her new role as wife and mother, meaning a business career will have to take a backseat in her list of priorities.

In retrospect, it's easy to see how Mike's original goal—to become president—was too ambitious. It's fine to have a vision for life, to think about what might happen, but a goal needs to be something you can act on, something immediately achievable. Mike had no clue about all the complex matters of life that could easily get in the way of his unrealistic goal. In fact, this is just what happened to John, whom we read about in the previous chapter. He eventually achieved his longtime goal of running a company, only to find it was not the right job for him.

As Denis Waitley writes in the *Joy of Working,* "Your goal should be just out of reach, but not out of sight."

The Problem of Goals That Are Too Unambitious

Setting goals too close, on the other hand—being overly conservative in order to avoid any semblance of risk or possibility of failure—will limit the progress we can achieve.

It is true that we can't possibly know all about our talents in our early years, but we do have some idea and sense about them. By the time we finish school, we should have a pretty good feel about them: We know where we excel. We know our strengths and weaknesses. We've learned that some extra effort on our part can offset advantages some others may have over us.

As we start out in life, we want to take advantage of what we already know about ourselves. We do that by setting some readily attainable goals that dovetail our interests and strengths. Then we should stretch ourselves and reach out a bit.

Start Small

In our first job, the initial goal should be to learn what is expected of us and to master any required skills and duties. If we want to advance, however, we must analyze how the job could be done better than in the past. We should then strive to make extra contributions to improve job performance.

We can also start looking at the position just above us, as well as other peer-level positions. What knowledge do we need to gain? What experience and skills are required to be promoted? Do we need special training or more education? Do we have the talent? What is the price to be paid? Are we willing to pay it? Are there other areas of the business that are more interesting and have a better future? What else is involved? How do we begin finding out?

This process of understanding all the answers does not happen overnight. It is a continual process of learning, applying, overcoming, evaluating, and persevering. Each step along the way is part of successful living. And this is a key point: Success is not something "way out there." Instead, we can be successful all of the time if we do our best and use our talents to their utmost each step along the way.

Sometimes we will see rapid progress, and at other times it will seem like our boots are stuck in the mud. Adversity is sure to rear its head, which may alter our direction in minor or major ways. (We will discuss adversity in greater depth later on. You will see how to deal with it in a positive way.)

Reevaluate Goals on a Regular Basis

As our base of values changes, so will our priorities and goals. This is not only natural but, more important, it is an essential part of successful living. If our base of values is the same at age forty-five as it was at age twenty-five, it suggests that a limited level of maturity has been attained. Fortunately, that is not the case for most of us.

If we accept the fact that our base of values will change over the years (and that our willingness to pay the price for achieving a goal is directly related to that base), then we should be reviewing our goals on a regular basis. If people set goals along a specific path and effectively apply the principles involved to attain them, then the chances are high that they will actually attain them or, at least, come close to actually achieving them. If goals are pursued blindly, however, without reassessment from time to time, the price that will be paid may be far more than they ever imagined.

Some people will pursue business goals simply in terms of position and income, neglecting such important aspects of their lives as family and friends. Even if these goals are achieved, they may suddenly discover that what was really important was missed along the way. That's why it's essential to reassess goals on a regular basis, checking them against our base of values and the various changes that have taken place in our lives. This will help us maintain a balanced life and keep our priorities in order.

As we discussed earlier, we cannot separate the idea of goal-setting from the principles of goal attainment. If we think about these two aspects in tandem, we realize that even as we set a goal, we will have to get unified in heart, mind, and words and be willing to pay a price. Finally, we will have to persevere in order to successfully achieve it.

That may mean we will have to experiment with our talents or accept a few setbacks along the way. I see these setbacks as opportunities, however—opportunities to learn and to grow. Yet many people will let adversity, setbacks, or even an occasional failure discourage them from setting other goals. They begin to doubt that they have the ability to accomplish anything in life, which keeps them from using talents they possess.

The reality is that most of us only use a very small percentage of the talents given to us by God. There are a lot of reasons for this, and I have already mentioned one of them—letting other people set goals for us. Let's take a look at some of the other major reasons.

We're Not Sure We Have Any Other Talents

Often we don't know—or we doubt—that we have any other talents than the ones we are now exercising. We live in a world where winning is everything and success is measured in terms of achievement. If we go along with that kind of thinking, it is easy to become deluded about our talents.

If we accept that excellence is the measuring stick for each talent we possess, then we're not going to risk trying something new if we cannot "excel" in it. How many of us never try new sports, study new subjects, dabble in painting, join a choir, volunteer for civic or charitable activities, or take on new responsibilities at work? Are we avoiding these other avenues of opportunity because we doubt that we have the talent to excel in these areas?

Too often we neglect trying new things because we don't

view them as opportunities to enrich our lives and the lives of others. We feel that if we can't do something perfectly from the very start, then that must mean we simply don't have the necessary talent.

We Are Afraid to Fail

This is a common reason many of us use only a small percentage of our talents. We accept someone else's standard of excellence and let it replace our standard of doing our best. We place so much importance on the approval of others that we tend to get cautious. We prefer not to take chances that would let us stand out in a crowd. This wrongheaded thinking can be extremely self-limiting.

Many of us, however, have a limited appreciation of how effectively we can develop our talents—or where they may lead us. Learning more about ourselves—and the old adage "It never hurts to try" applies here—is a positive and stimulating process. Who cares if we fail? Failing often happens any number of times before we reach new levels of talent usage and accomplishment.

Too many of us let life slip by in a numbing fashion, letting routine become the norm. We don't step out and explore new territories. Consider the remarkable accomplishments of some people who stepped out of their comfort zones. Albert Schweitzer, the noted physician, didn't earn his medical degree until he was well past middle age. Grandma Moses didn't start painting seriously until she was seventy-eight years old. Colonel Sanders of Kentucky Fried Chicken fame didn't start sharing his finger-lickin' recipe until he was sixty-six years old.

These people became well known, but there are countless others—ordinary people living in ordinary towns—who are successfully exploiting untapped talents at all ages. People take up tennis, begin walking programs, join reading or bridge clubs, start new careers after retirement, or get involved in charitable and civic activities. A woman doesn't have to be a great athlete to learn how to swing a golf club. If her husband likes the game, she can learn to play it and share meaningful and enjoyable time with him.

If a particular job is not satisfying, then try developing other skills that can open up new opportunities and new career directions. The possibility of failure should not prevent us from discovering a host of talents we have overlooked.

We Quit before the Race Is Over

I mentioned earlier that commitment to a goal involves paying a price. Since it is often difficult to fully appreciate what that price might be, we often get disillusioned when it turns out to be higher than we thought. We can also run into those temporary setbacks or unexpected adversities. While these events are not unusual when developing talent, they can be discouraging. We begin to doubt ourselves and play up the negative aspects. Once we become unwilling to pay the price, the original goal is lost.

The first order of business in those situations is to immediately reassess our base of values. If the price to be paid is higher than we first anticipated, then we have to evaluate our willingness to pay it. If a stumbling block appears, then we have to look for ways of overcoming it. This can work for our benefit, because in the process we learn more about our talent.

What we are doing is reevaluating our goal and determining our desire to commit ourselves toward its achievement. It's a personal decision, of course, and sometimes it becomes clear that we started out on the wrong road. More often, however, it's only a temporary setback, and if we learn from it, we're back on the right track.

We Delay Taking Action

This is a common reason that so many people do not take advantage of their talents. We all have various dreams and desires, but we often just keep putting off the goal-setting process and the action required to achieve our goals. If we do that, we are in danger of losing our "now" focus, which can stall any success we will attain.

As a simple example, hardly anyone starts a diet on a Thursday or Friday. After all, the weekend is coming. Wouldn't it make more sense to start a diet on Monday? But then the weekend comes and goes and it's Monday morning. Guess what? Our resolve has weakened. *Well, I can always diet later this week.* Then it's Thursday again and the diet is put off again. And on and on it goes.

This pattern of not following through, whether it's dieting, learning a foreign language, taking a computer course, or whatever, is all too common in people's lives. They would like to do new things, try out new talents, and pursue a dream, but somehow that first step never materializes.

It's human nature to take the path of least resistance. It's easy to let another evening slip away in front of the television rather than taking action—action that achievement demands.

Stepping Out

As we review the principles for setting goals and then look at the reasons we may not be applying them, we should think again of the "now" focus. It's never too early—and never too late—to make changes in our lives. We all have the same "now." Begin by taking time out to see where you are. Have you fallen into the habit of letting things drift? Have you stopped experimenting and stepping out into some new areas of growth?

If the daily routine has you thinking that life is passing you by, it's not too late to take control and bring about change. In all likelihood, you have more talent than you think. Do your best, and you will find new areas for achievement and for positive interactions with your family, friends, and associates.

SECRET #3

Pay the Price

In the last chapter, we looked at the necessary components to setting good life goals. One of these, being willing to pay a price, is actually important enough that it stands alone as one of the six secrets to success. A pivotal experience in my own life helped me to learn the principle of paying the price. It also illustrates an important point relative to expanding the use of our talents. In my case, it was not a particularly significant talent—but I'm glad I didn't let concerns about my ability to excel deter me from tapping a previously unused talent and pursuing my goal.

A Striking Discovery

It all started when I was in my early teens and first discovered girls. Oh, they had always been around, of course, but suddenly they caught my attention in an entirely new way. This turn of events presented a quandary: How was I going to meet them, get to know them, and impress them?

Unfortunately, my self-esteem and self-image in regard to the opposite sex were not at high levels. For one thing, my experience with them was very limited. I had two brothers but no sisters, and I attended an all-boys school. Although I was active in sports and various school activities, most of my experience was being gained in primarily masculine environments.

My family was reasonably affluent, and after I was in high school we started spending each summer at a beach community. There were a lot of boys and girls there and lots of opportunities to meet and mix with attractive young ladies. Even then, however, I felt at a disadvantage because my fair skin easily sunburned. I was also self-conscious about the freckles that resulted.

As you might suspect, I cast about trying to find some way to stand out a bit and to somehow become attractive to all of these lovely maidens who were regularly passing me by. My progress was very slow. Then one evening at a party, where I stood with some other fellows in the same predicament, a boy about my own age began to play the piano.

Over the years, I have noted many reasons why people experiment and begin to use previously untapped talents. Frequently, it relates to career advancement—ambition can be a strong motivator. Some people will step out of their safety zones to fulfill a need in their lives, while others do it to please a parent, a spouse, or another family member. Many people will try new things just for the fun of it. Regardless of the reasons, however, the results can often yield surprising benefits far beyond the original expectations.

I really can't tell you today how well that boy at the party played the piano, but at that particular moment it sounded great. He knew all the popular songs and, as he played, a number of girls flocked around to listen and sing. My mind was made up. I would learn to play the piano.

Now, actually, the piano was a touchy subject in our house. When my older brother, Bob, was about nine or ten, my mother had decided he should learn the piano. He really didn't want to and he really didn't like it, but in our home, likes and dislikes on the part of children did not play an important role in decision-making. So, Bob started lessons—and, along with them, started the daily squabbles to make him practice. Mother was adamant and Father supported her—as long as practicing was completed before he arrived home from work.

When my turn came a few years later, Mother simply wasn't up to another piano fight. Instead, she had come across an old family mandolin in the attic, and this was promptly assigned to me.

Have you ever played a mandolin? Ever heard one played? Mandolins may be a romantic instrument—I always pictured a gondolier in Venice strumming his cherrywood mandolin on a moonlit night—but I quickly learned that on this side of the Atlantic, mandolins do not set a young girl's heart fluttering.

Regardless, my mother was not about to budge just because a son moaned regularly about playing the stupid mandolin. Grudgingly, I learned to play the instrument.

But now, learning to play the piano was my objective. No one was forcing me to do it. I wanted to. So, I began.

Picking out melodies with one finger on my right hand was fairly easy because the music notes were the same for both the mandolin and piano. Unfortunately, I couldn't read the music for the left hand, so I faked that part. The result was noise. While this didn't discourage me, it irritated my mother and father to no end. Now the squabbles increased as they tried to make Bob practice and to make me stop.

It was obvious to me, of course, that I needed a teacher. Listening to the classical music my brother was playing after seven years, however, chilled me. At fourteen, I was a young man in a hurry. As I saw it, in seven years I would be old and all of the girls would be gone. I knew there had to be a better way.

I located the boy who had played at the party, and he told me he had only started a year earlier and had learned by the chord method. He explained that you keep rhythm with the left hand, playing chords that vary depending on the key in which the song was written. I didn't understand much of what he was telling me, but I did find out his teacher's name.

Convincing my parents to let me take lessons was easier than I had expected because my incessant noise had brought them to the point that whenever I sat at the piano, they were forced to other parts of the house. My father had even started referring to our basement as his living room.

So the lessons began, and gradually, slowly but steadily, I learned the rudiments of piano playing. Then finally came the day when the chords I was playing with my left hand came together with the melody flowing from my right hand. The result was music!

Looking back now, it is evident that I had established a goal and was totally committed to achieving it. From the outset, I was perfectly willing to pay the price for learning to play. I was committed, and the time that had to be allocated for practice, practice, and more practice was no great sacrifice.

In some cases, of course, once you consider the cost of your goal you may realize it is more than you are willing to pay. For instance, a number of years after I had mastered the fundamentals of piano playing, I realized that there was a greater price to be paid if I wished to advance further. At that point, I decided that the small additional gain to be had was not worth what it would have cost me in time and effort. But I've always been glad I made that initial investment and developed this hidden talent.

A Valuable New Skill

A few years ago, I was in Europe on business and found myself with a free weekend. A couple of friends suggested we travel to the Côte d'Azur—the famed French Riviera. On Saturday morning, we made the short flight to Nice, that lovely resort city located on the coast of the Mediterranean Sea. We checked in at one of the many hotels that overlook the busy boardwalk and well-groomed beach.

After a pleasant day, we dined in the hotel restaurant and enjoyed the kind of five-course dinner that only the French can serve. As the dessert and coffee reached our table, I heard the sound of a piano coming from the nearby lounge. When the meal was completed, we walked over to listen.

Seated at the piano was a handsome young man with a flashing smile. Accompanying him on the bass fiddle was an older man. The striking resemblance between the two suggested that they were father and son.

We struck up a friendly conversation with them between sets and, indeed, they were *père et fils*—Jean-Claude and his son, Pierre. When they played, I stood close to the piano studying Pierre's technique, the way he arranged songs, and the fill-ins he used to enhance the melodies.

After an hour or so, Pierre said he had some phone calls to make, so he invited me to play while he was away. I hesitated, but Jean-Claude insisted. It turned out to be great fun.

It is always an asset to have another rhythm instrument such as a bass fiddle or drums accompanying you when you play the piano. Jean-Claude was a real pro, shifting chords easily regardless of the songs I played and maintaining a solid beat. We played a medley of popular American songs, and as we did, a number of young men and women came and stood nearby, tapping their feet and moving with the music.

I thought back to being fourteen again and that early goal I had set and had achieved. I reflected on how much pleasure the piano had brought and what an extra asset it had been over the years. I played with small bands during college years and, besides having fun, even made extra spending money. During the early years of my marriage, I supplemented our income by playing with small bands at parties, and sometimes playing solo when big bands took breaks at larger affairs.

As the years passed, playing the piano became an integral part of our family life with our children—and now with our grandchildren.

Playing that night in Nice was a nice reminder of how much

I would have missed if I had failed to step out and develop a simple talent. But I wanted to, remember?

To get the most out of a talent, even if some outside pressure forces you to try something new, there has to be that point where you make the decision that you "want to." You know the cost of your commitment, and despite that cost, you have the want-to that compels you to pay the price.

Based on my results, when my younger brother, Milt, reached the age of ten, my mother started him on what turned out to be five years of piano lessons. He hated them just as much as Bob had when he was forced to take lessons. Neither of my brothers reached a point where they *wanted* to play the piano, and neither ever played again.

The same is true of me and that stupid mandolin.

Discover the Law of Reciprocity

Up to this point, we have been dealing primarily with "what to do" factors for successful living. We have given consideration to getting a "now" focus in our lives, to effectively setting and attaining goals, and to being willing to pay the price of expanding on the various talents God has given us.

In addition, we have already seen that material success doesn't necessarily guarantee happiness, contentment, and peace of mind—which are our ultimate goals. Many people, including the achievers in today's society, lead lives filled with disappointment, disillusionment, and frustration. Why is that? The answer can be boiled down to this statement: It is not just *what* we do, but *how* we do it that makes the difference.

These "how" factors not only affect the degree of our achievements, but they also bear directly on the quality of our achievements, because it is in how we do things that the fruits of success are found.

A Basis in Law

This brings us face-to-face with another great law of the universe—the law of reciprocity.

On the surface, this is a simple law—and so common that just about everybody knows it. We learned it as children when we were taught the Golden Rule: "Do unto others as you would have them do unto you." These days in many quarters, quoting Scripture is not politically correct, so the Bible's teaching that you reap what you sow translates into this modern-day prose: What goes around, comes around. Either way, you see the point.

In the physical realm, a manifestation of the law of reciprocity is "For every action there is an equal and opposite reaction." You don't have to be a student of nuclear physics to realize there is such a law, even though you might not be able to understand its full implications.

Let's break this concept down. We know, for example, that it takes energy to lift, pull, or push something. We know that force is required to overcome resistance. We know that we use the law of reciprocity when we walk, run, or swim.

Now let's apply the law of reciprocity to personal relationships. When we are nice to people, they tend to be nice to us. When we are rude or nasty, people tend to give us a taste of our own medicine. In other words, the way we conduct ourselves with other people generally bears directly on how they will conduct themselves with us. Keep in mind that we interrelate with other people nearly all of the time.

All of these people, in one way or another, impact our lives—just as we impact theirs. It is essential to understand that in every personal relationship, the law of reciprocity is at work. Because of that, the law is either working for us or against us. More than any other factor, the failure to understand this correlation—and letting the law work against us—is responsible for the problems that so many people face.

While most of us accept the fact that there is a law of reciprocity, we don't necessarily think about it a great deal or give much consideration to its real depth and gravity. But generally speaking, most of us would agree that it is better to be nice than nasty. Most of us would say that we are not out to get the other guy, and we believe in things like honesty and fair play.

Yet these are just platitudes for many of us, and when push comes to shove, we are prone to look out for number one. All too often, we pay lip service to "doing unto others as we would have them do unto us." Actually, we are more prone to operate on the principle of "do unto others before they do unto us." It's all too easy for our concerns, our progress, our achievements, our interests, and our comforts to become the priorities in our lives.

Such an attitude can develop easily in today's competitive world. It may seem to be the best choice we have. The reality, however, is that such an attitude is not the only choice that we have. In fact, when we make the choice to pursue self-interest, we will eventually run into problems.

So why do we so frequently fail in our understanding and use of the law of reciprocity?

We Get It Backwards

Simply stated, the law of reciprocity states that you give and then you receive. It implies that the more you give, the more you get. Taken a step further, the amount and the quality of what you receive is measured and defined by what you give.

Unfortunately, human nature being what it is, many of us try to turn this law on its head. We want to *get* first, then we plan to *give* in return. We see this attitude in the workplace all the time. Employees ask for raises on the basis that they will work harder or more efficiently. We see it when a husband tells his wife that he will take her out more if she fixes better meals or keeps the house neater. We hear children promise to do their homework and get better grades if they can have their own computer.

I could list more examples, but perhaps you might take a moment to think of the occasions you have done this as well. The problem is that we all want to get, but all too often we hold back on what we will give until we get what we want. When we do this, we have not changed the law of reciprocity at all. The law will simply work against us. Our actions will limit what we receive in any given situation.

As you look around at people, ask yourself if the individuals are "givers" or "takers." A clearer way to think of it is to take a measuring tape with "giver" at one end and "taker" at the other. We all probably fall somewhere in the middle because none of us is totally a giver. Why is that? Because none of us is perfect.

I doubt, however, that there are many 100 percent takers as well. Even the worst of us needs to be nice to someone at least part of the time. Perhaps the worst case is the story of a cynical man who says he takes advantage of everyone he can—"except for six friends, whom I'm saving for my pallbearers."

Let's face it. We are all givers or takers at various times. Where we fall in the range between all giving and all taking, however, determines to what degree we have the law of reciprocity working for or against us.

In marriage, for example, two people who are high on the taker side haven't got a chance. Their marriage will become a battleground with constant conflict. For them, separation or divorce is just a matter of time.

If, on the other hand, one spouse is a giver and the other a taker, the marriage may work, but it all depends on the degree of giving and taking. How long will the giver keep on giving? Since even the giver in that relationship is not always a giver, conflict will arise sooner or later. More important, love is given little space to grow and flourish. This is one reason why many marriages break up after fifteen or twenty years.

If you look at a solid marriage, whether it be of a few years or fifty years, you will always find two people who are both on the "giver" side of the range. While neither is perfect, each has a deep concern about the care and well-being of the other. One may be more of a dominant personality, but deep down, they both try to look out for each other, to please and support.

In this atmosphere, love and dependency deepen. The two truly become one, and the law of reciprocity functions to their advantage. They are each giving, and they are each getting.

The law works this way in all areas of our lives. Our attitude should be: Giving is first, getting is second. Consider what happens in the workplace. We pay our dues first. We learn the job. We apply ourselves. We give our best effort, offering our skills to the company's benefit. When we perform well, we begin to see returns in the form of promotions and pay raises.

This is the way life works, and despite a few people who seem to make it work in reverse (taking first, then giving), we should not be fooled. Getting the law backward will work against us.

We Use the Law in a Shallow Way

Years ago, I read Dale Carnegie's book *How to Win Friends and Influence People*. Carnegie's book was so popular at one time that the book title became part of the American vernacular. I read the book early in my business career, and it provided many insights about the importance of developing fruitful relationships with people.

The key point that I took away from *How to Win Friends and Influence People* was that I should tone down my own ego to focus more on other people's needs. By understanding others better and catering to their concerns, I could have a more positive impact on them. The kicker is that I would then reap greater results—both professionally and personally.

I took Carnegie's advice to heart as I steadily progressed in my career. There were times, of course, when I wished my colleagues had also read the book—so they would cater a bit more to me. It seemed that I was being the giver, and they were always the takers. Still, I used the book's principles to my advantage for a fair period of time.

Many years later, however, it dawned on me that my understanding of the book's thesis was, in fact, quite shallow. Instead of really caring about people, I was actually trying to manipulate them for my own advantage. This superficial understanding and application of the law of reciprocity produced its own reaction. I was giving only superficially, and that became the measure of the results I achieved. People tended to see through my superficiality, and it wasn't long before many began to sense that I was manipulating them for my own benefit.

This is what I finally learned: The law of reciprocity has two sides—the action (giving) side and the reaction (getting) side. We greatly limit the benefits of the law if our intent is to control both sides of the equation. It becomes self-defeating if we are giving only in terms of what we want to get.

Yet, all too many people do just that. They give specifically to get, but more important, they want the equation balanced each time. For instance, they do a favor for someone and expect a favor back. They attach strings to everything they do. They look for gratitude, for applause, for the tangible returns that seem only fair when they do things for other people.

These people fail to see the shallowness of this type of giving. They are, in effect, always trying to balance the scales for their own benefit. Such an approach misses the real point of the law of reciprocity, and it will inevitably lead to many disappointments down the road. They will see people fail to respond in the way they expect or even demand.

We Use the Law Selectively

A very common reason many of us fail to attain the full benefits of the law of reciprocity is that we tend to use it selectively. We see its advantages, and, even more important, we recognize the necessity of using the law in certain situations with certain people. But we don't think much about it in other situations or with other people. Although this may well provide positive results for us, the overall impact of the law is working against us, and it will inevitably create problems in the future.

A man starting a new job, for example, realizes that he must please his superior to get ahead in the company. This means it is important to respond positively to his boss's directions and conduct himself in a way designed to gain his or her approval.

This man will also try to determine who else is important in the company—either higher-level managers or peers whose acceptance and approval are important to his future with the company. At the same time, however, he may be identifying others in the organization who, in his view, are less important to his success. These people, he has decided, can be used to his advantage.

I've seen many business careers ruined or take sharp detours because people have done this very sort of thing. You never know when there will be changes in management, shifts in board control, or even changes in ownership. If you are clearly identified with the group suddenly out of power, you may find yourself viewed negatively by the very people you were ignoring or treating poorly.

Another common example is the Jekyll and Hyde individual—the person who is pleasant, cooperative, and productive at work and mean-spirited, dominating, and unloving at home. Any frustrations that were swallowed at work rise to the surface and explode within the confines of home. This type of person is using the law of reciprocity selectively, and while his career side may flourish, his family life is crumbling quickly. The marriage is headed for bitterness, estrangement, or even divorce.

Unfortunately, many of us selectively use the law of reciprocity in our lives. We don't really understand its depth and the fact that it's always working for or against us. People who are polite and helpful when it is to their advantage—but are rude and self-serving when they believe they can get away with it—are playing a dangerous game with the law. In one form or another, the time will come when those negative actions will come back to haunt them. They are courting disaster.

We Try to Ignore the Law

Despite the overwhelming evidence that ignoring the law often leads to disastrous results, many people still try to live as if the law of reciprocity doesn't apply to them. In other words, they believe they are above the law.

We all have met someone who seems to get away with flouting the law. Often, they have achieved significant levels of material success despite their self-centered attitude and actions. We know people way over on the "taker" side who are reaching high levels of position, power, and money. At the same time, we know many "givers" who are passed by, pushed aside, and appear to be living unrewarding lives.

Ah, but there are two major realities about this seeming imbalance. The first is that appearances can be deceiving. If we consider only the material definition of success, then yes, there are many people who have achieved it through self-centered, opportunistic, and "taking" actions that fly in the face of the law of reciprocity.

To say that they haven't paid a price for their fruits of success, however, is simply not true. One need only read their biographies, particularly the "unauthorized" ones, to learn of the unhappiness they have caused themselves and others along the way. A string of broken marriages, alienated friends, and plotting enemies are left in the wake. While they may have lived the lifestyles of the rich and famous, sooner or later they will learn how shallow their achievements have been. If they haven't, it's because they are too busy pursuing more and more pleasure. And the cycle never stops.

Appearances are also deceiving for the givers of the world. Many givers never reach the level of material success attained by the takers. While they may lack some of life's tangible luxuries or even struggle with financial hardship, many are still enjoying the fruits of success. In fact, they are content to enjoy life's simple pleasures. They can wake up each morning knowing that they are doing their best with the talents they possess. The are also experiencing happiness in family life and friendships.

The second reality about the law is that we live in an imperfect world. Through no fault of our own, we can be mugged in the street or get struck by a drunk driver. We can be passed over for a promotion or even lose our job. We can be cheated or taken advantage of in a thousand different situations, which seems to invalidate the law.

Despite these paradoxes, however, the law of reciprocity does work, and ultimately it works perfectly. In the end, the scales will be balanced evenly. To understand this concept, we must first grasp the full depth and gravity of the law. This can only be seen when we look at the spiritual side of our lives.

God and the Law of Reciprocity

We all agree that the law works in the physical realm. When there's an action, there is always a reaction. We also agree that the law of reciprocity generally works on the interpersonal level. It may not seem to work perfectly on that level because some of us are givers, while some of us are takers. And, we know some people will rebuff us no matter how nice we are to them.

We are also aware that the results of the law are affected by the position and power of the people with whom we are interacting. For example, if we are rude to a store clerk or a waitress, the effect of such rudeness will probably be far less than if we act the same way with our boss. If you really want to see some negative effects from rude behavior, try snubbing the president of your company the next time you see him in the hallway!

Conversely, when we are polite, positive, and a team player, the rewards will also be influenced by the position and power of the people with whom we are interrelating. This is reflected in what those people can do for us.

The full implication of this becomes apparent only when we realize that the law of reciprocity applies to the spiritual realm. It is, in fact, the same law. In the spiritual realm, we must be aware that we are not dealing on a person-to-person basis but, far more important, on a person-to-God basis.

Think about it: It is God himself who established the law. It is always in effect; it is unchangeable; and it will always balance out perfectly. In our relationship with God, we are dealing with the Creator. It is not simply that he has power but, rather, that he *is* the power.

In creating us, however, God gave us free will. We make the choices—poor, indifferent, or good. We can choose to believe or not believe, to obey or not obey. He has given us control over the first part of the law—what we sow—but he has the ultimate control over the second part—what we reap.

If we look at the negative side first, we've already pointed out that in dealing on a person-to-person basis, the level of response to a negative action is limited by the power and position of the person with whom we are dealing. When we look at the spiritual realm, however, we should see that an action against an infinite being will in turn call for an infinite response.

In this regard, the Bible states that "the wages of sin is death" (Romans 6:23). Since we all sin, it is apparent that without some sort of intervention we would have no way of avoiding the spiritual consequences of our actions. The law of reciprocity would work against us, and, left to our own resources, we would reap the consequences, which would ultimately be separation from God for all eternity.

Fortunately for us, however, God chose to intervene. This is why the gospel is referred to as the "Good News." God sent his only Son as Savior to the world. He who was sinless, Jesus

Christ, took on all of our sins and paid the penalty for them, and he offers that sacrifice to each of us as a free gift.

When we accept it, the spiritual consequences of our sins are nullified, and the scales are perfectly balanced. Our sins are washed away when we accept him, and they continue to be washed away, even when we fall from time to time. Now let's review the complete verse from Romans 6:23: "For the wages of sin is death, but the free gift of God is eternal life in Christ Jesus our Lord."

While we are saved from the spiritual consequences, however, we cannot always avoid the worldly consequences of our sinful behavior. If we steal, we may go to jail. If we cheat on our spouse, cut corners in our business dealings, take advantage of people, or yield to other temptations, the consequences will have to be faced. Whenever we step out of the will of God, we open ourselves up to negative forces and negative results.

But we should concentrate on the positive side of the law. When we are dealing on a person-to-God basis, our godly thoughts, words, and actions also call for an infinite response. The scales will be balanced on the positive side as well. Because we live in an imperfect world, we may not always reap the full benefits of our positive actions during our lifetime, but it's comforting to know they have infinite and eternal value.

Money and the Law of Reciprocity

When thinking of the law of reciprocity in regard to our relationship with God, there is one other area we should consider. Many Christians do not seem to grasp the significance of giving and getting when it comes to money.

In the Old Testament, it is clear that God demanded that his people tithe—give ten percent—from the firstfruits of their labor. When Jesus came, however, he did not use the term tithing, but rather he emphasized the law of reciprocity. In Luke 6:38, Jesus says: "Give, and it will be given to you; good measure, pressed down, shaken together, running over, they will pour into your lap. For by your standard of measure it will be measured to you in return." Can you see the significance of this? He changed a legalistic obligation into an opportunity. Unfortunately, many Christians view this as an opportunity to give less, rather than more, to God's work. The bottom line is that they are cheating themselves.

There are two points I want to emphasize regarding giving. Rather than imposing a legalism on us, Jesus is looking for loving hearts. He put it on a personal basis when he told us that whatever we do for the least of his brothers, we do for him (Matthew 25:40).

The second point is that we cannot make deals with God. If our objective is to control both sides of the equation with our giving, then it won't work. God knows our motives and our hearts. A give-to-get scenario will never be blessed by God.

Feeding the poor, helping the needy, reaching out to single-parent families, and supporting various ministries are all opportunities for giving. If our motivations are sincere, if we give out of a sense of love, caring, and compassion, then we have his word that we will be blessed. But he may not choose to bless us financially because he knows what is best for us. What we have to do is leave the second half of the equation to God.

In my own experience, as well as that of many friends and acquaintances I've met over the years, God often does choose to give back in financial terms. I am convinced that many Christians go through life always on the edge of financial disaster simply because they don't give enough. They don't seem to grasp that we have God's own word that he will honor us for our compassion and generosity—that's a promise from Scripture.

Applying the Law of Reciprocity to Real Life

Paul, a wealthy man, is chairman of a large chemicals company. Starting with his first job out of college, he calculated each move he would have to make to advance rapidly. During the next twenty years he changed companies twice, each time broadening his responsibilities and increasing his income substantially. As he climbed the management ladder, however, his focus on getting to the top led him to adopt an attitude of aloofness with his subordinates.

As Paul's income steadily increased, he retained skilled financial advisors to invest his money wisely. But he became suspicious of people with smaller financial portfolios than his own and began limiting his social life to those he considered his equals. Meanwhile, Paul also became annoyed with various people and charitable groups that, in his mind, wanted to take advantage of his growing wealth. It seemed like every week he was asked to contribute to a Junior League fund-raising event, to the United Way, or some other charitable organization.

That's not where Paul had his focus. Over a period of years, he was far more interested in making his money grow and preserving his investments for the future. He was not even aware that his earlier bent of generosity and concern for others had been gradually diminishing.

On the marital front, Paul and his first wife divorced after fifteen years of marriage. While he felt moments of remorse, he rationalized them away by telling himself that his former wife simply didn't share his interests and ambitions. Furthermore, she hadn't really seemed to fit in with the people he admired.

So Paul went out and found a "trophy" wife—a younger and more stylish woman who shared his social ambition. She gave expensive parties, and they were invited regularly to the top social affairs.

Following one of their parties, when the guests had left and he had retired to his study, Paul suddenly realized how empty his life had become. As he sat back in a comfortable chair, it occurred to him that there had not been any real friends at the party. They were just people, very much like himself, coming together to fill empty hours.

The conversations were, for the most part, meaningless and impersonal. Closer to home, Paul was shocked to realize that he didn't really share anything of importance with his wife, Susan—and she certainly didn't share herself with him. Paul felt depressed, and feelings of loneliness swept over him.

While loneliness is more common in older people, its causes are often found in the way people live their lives in their younger years. It is then they are "sowing" what they will later "reap." Another case in point is Julia.

She is in her mid-thirties, married to a lawyer, and has two lovely children. Julia leads an active life, plays tennis several times a week, and has a full social calendar. If you asked her if she was happy and fulfilled, she would be startled by the question. Of course she would say yes, but the reality is that she's traveling rapidly along a path that could lead to loneliness and disappointment.

In this instance the key to Julia's present life is her husband, an attractive, likable, and popular man. He is a caring person, and people are drawn to him like a magnet. He sees Julia as a beautiful woman and indulges her every whim.

Julia, on the other hand, is a self-centered person who likes to run the show. She exhibits a somewhat superior attitude with people she considers to be socially lower than herself, including waitresses, sales clerks, and other service employees. She is unaware that many of her "friends" only put up with her because of their fondness for her husband.

Remember, we reap what we sow. But another aspect of the law is that we reap in proportion to what we sow. If we get the law of reciprocity backwards in our personal relationships (or use it selectively or in a shallow or negative way), we are establishing the nature of those relationships later in life.

If we look objectively, we will see that the major problem

for most people is not so much found in what they sow as it is in the *amount* they sow. One way to look at it is to consider our lives as if we each started out with one hundred acres of fertile ground. In our barn are dozens and dozens of seed bags. Most of it is good seed, but there are a few bad bags of seed mixed in.

We know that most people do try to sow good seed most of the time. Paul and Julia are not "bad" people—they aren't thieves, murderers, or drug dealers—but most of the time they aren't sowing anything. They spread some good seed from time to time, and they also toss some bad seed into the fields as well. Most of their acreage, however, doesn't get any seed at all.

Planting a Garden

What we want to do first is to think in terms of what we want to reap. If we *know* what we want to reap, then we will know what we want to sow.

If we were planting a garden, for example, we might decide to plant zinnias in one area, tulips in another, and rose bushes in the back row. Whatever we wanted to grow would dictate what we would plant. We would also be aware that we would have to cultivate, water, and weed the plant beds so the flowers could bloom in fullness. We would also know, of course, that if we left parts of the garden unplanted, we could not expect any flowers to grow in those areas.

When we convert this analogy to the way we live, we realize that if we want love, we have to *plant* love. If we want friendship, we have to *plant* friendship. Compassion begets compassion. Kindness begets kindness. Concern for others begets concern for ourselves. Just as surely, discord will beget discord. In order for us to reap the full benefits of what we sow, we will have to cultivate, water, and take care of any weeds that crop up from time to time.

Another important step in getting the law of reciprocity to work in our favor is to reduce the "self-focus" in our lives.

When we focus on ourselves, we see events primarily in terms of how they affect us rather than seeing them objectively, learning from them, and seizing the opportunities they may present.

Similarly, "self-focus" limits our ability to develop meaningful personal relationships with others. We are perceived as self-centered, and we find our lack of interest in others being reciprocated. Self-focus is also a fertile ground for the growth of emotional problems, such as self-pity, poor self-image, and all types of anxieties and fears.

It is very difficult to develop meaningful relationships with people if we let these emotional problems grow in our lives. Rather, we have to start looking outward—seeing other people as people. It's easy to forget that others have feelings, concerns, ambitions, hopes, and dreams just as we do. They are our neighbors. They have families and loved ones. They laugh and cry and struggle just like us. They are important.

Finally, as we see people for themselves, we have to start caring about them. We want to start smiling and talking to them. Most important, we have to listen to them. As we develop relationships with others, we have to share with them—share their concerns, their joys, their achievements, and their failures. Equally important, we have to share some of ourselves and let them know that we are vulnerable too. Regardless of our age or our station in life, it is never too late to have the law of reciprocity work for us. When we do, the rewards can be amazing.

The Right Attitude

I have a California friend of thirty years who has had the law of reciprocity working full-tilt in his favor for a long time. Dave is in his early eighties now, and his wife passed away about ten years ago. Her death was a sorrowful time for him, but the seeds he had planted throughout his life came into full bloom when he needed them most. His family and friends were there for him—and they continue to be there.

I talk with Dave from time to time, and during our conversations, he generally mentions a number of our mutual acquaintances who have been in touch or visited with him in recent months. One evening not long ago, we had dinner in Los Angeles and reminisced about past times we had shared. We recalled a particular evening we had taken our wives to a nice restaurant, followed by a show on Sunset Boulevard.

As we sat there talking about his wife, I noticed Dave's eyes mist over for a moment. "I still miss Marion quite a bit," he confided, "but time has a way of healing things like that."

I asked Dave if he ever felt lonely.

He seemed surprised by my question.

"No, not lonely," he answered thoughtfully. "My life is full. I still have my children, of course, and then the grandchildren and even a couple of great-grandchildren. I visit friends regularly and keep in touch. I am really too busy to be lonely."

He paused a moment. "Of course," he continued, "there are times when no one's around, and my health problems are starting to show up more frequently. Every so often I find myself experiencing self-pity. But I know the way to take care of that. I have the Lord and his Word. Getting into the Bible gets me back on track pretty fast. Then I realize I am never alone."

I watched Dave lean forward, his eyes alight with interest.

"Now tell me," he said, "what you have been doing since we last talked? And tell me all about Martha and your children."

Wasn't that nice? That's the way Dave is—never wanting to dwell on himself. That's the way I've always known him. He has always minimized "self-focus" in his life and shown a lively and sincere interest in others. He looks for the best in everyone he meets. I always feel better after I've been with him.

Dave built a strong support system during his life. He not only did it in his relationships with others, but he also did it in his relationship with Jesus. His life is a prime example of the fruit of the law of reciprocity.

Many of us do not have Dave's outgoing personality. But that doesn't matter. In Jesus, we have an understanding and always-present friend. He loves us just the way we are, and he can fill any emptiness we may have. We may require more help than Dave does, but Jesus knows that, and he can meet all of our needs.

No, my good friend Dave isn't lonely. No one really has to be.

SECRET #5
Develop a Winning Attitude

Our attitude or mental outlook plays a major role in virtually everything we do. It affects the quality of our achievements, our relationships with everyone with whom we come into contact, and our overall enjoyment of life.

Regardless of career path, our attitude will affect our progress in either a positive or a negative way. It is the first thing that employers look for, starting with that first employment interview. They continue to react to it after we are on the job. Co-workers notice it also, and it will have a major effect on the relationships we establish with them and with other people at all levels in the company.

If our work involves contacts with customers or clients our attitude will also affect the results we achieve with them. Since our attitude has a number of aspects to it, people we deal with aren't as much analyzing it as they are reacting to it. Again, it will be either in a positive or negative way.

One of the objectives of this book is to show "what" to do in order to make the most effective use of our talents. Attitude is another of those "how" factors that either help us or hinder us in accomplishing that. It is so important that we want to understand clearly the various aspects that make up our overall attitude as we deal with a great variety of problems and opportunities each day. To do our best and to be our best we have to be sure we have the right attitude. Perhaps it could best be described as a "winning" attitude. Let's break down the various traits of a winning attitude and look at them individually.

An Upbeat Demeanor

Think for a moment of some people you really like. You enjoy talking with them on the phone or running into them and sharing for a few minutes. When you call them, there is sort of a lilt in their voice when you identify yourself over the telephone. They are obviously glad to hear from you, and you know it. Their eyes light up when you meet, and a feeling of pleasure fills you.

These are upbeat people. You don't normally analyze it, but you feel it and you like it. You enjoy being with them. The focus of upbeat people is outgoing and friendly. They affect those around them in a positive way. They find a zest to life and they transmit it to others.

Developing this trait of a "winning" attitude requires an act of will. You have a choice when you wake in the morning, and you will have choice after choice during the day. Why not start the day greeting the Lord with joy and thanksgiving? Another day with its opportunities and challenges. How about a cheery "Good morning" and a kiss for your spouse? You will start his or her day a lot better than with a doleful expression or a gripe about it being Monday morning again. You will already have started the day primed to do your best.

A good example of upbeat attitudes can be found in talk show hosts on radio and television. We have no way of knowing, of course, whether they are the same way in the other parts of their lives, but they understand the importance of being upbeat during their shows. I'm sure that in those last few minutes before they go on stage they consciously prime themselves to project a warm, friendly, and upbeat attitude. It's essential for their success.

It is also a very important factor in our success regardless of our type of work. An upbeat attitude is a very positive factor for all of us. It may be hard to sustain at first, but keep at it and you will find the amazing benefits that can result.

A Positive Approach

This trait can best be illustrated by thinking about those people we all know who have negative attitudes. They can see problems in almost any situation. If you tell them you want to lose weight and mention the diet you plan to follow, they shake their heads and let you know quickly that it won't work very well, or even if it does, that you will probably put the pounds back on.

If sales in your company are off, the negative people seem to know all the reasons. They can list them in detail, but rarely will you hear a solution from them or a plan of attack that will turn the situation around. If others suggest possible solutions, they find faults with every one of them.

When someone suggests a solution to a particular problem, of course, it may not be the best or correct one. But a person with a positive attitude will strive to find the good in it and build on it. When a group of positive people brainstorm together, they build on each other's ideas and, more often than not, a solid plan emerges.

A positive attitude sees victory, not defeat. It is virtually impossible to achieve a goal with a negative attitude. As we showed earlier, commitment to a goal requires being unified in mind, heart, and word, and this requires a positive attitude. Our progress in the business world or in any other field of endeavor will be faster and more noteworthy if we approach problems and go after each goal with a positive, can-do attitude. It's what distinguishes the winners from the losers.

An Outgoing Personality

People who are outgoing tend to keep a tight rein on "self-focus." Instead, they are interested in the people with whom they interrelate, and they look for the good in them.

Early in my career as an executive recruiter, my major focus was on finding suitable candidates to fill positions for the clients who were paying me to do just that. It is still my objective in any search, but my attitude toward the people I interview has changed.

It is always necessary to personally interview potential candidates. Résumés of their background, or even the telephone discussions that determine preliminary interest, do not allow for true evaluation of their experience or the personal qualities necessary to meet the client's expectations.

In a personal interview it does not take very long to know if a candidate is not qualified. It takes a lot longer to determine that an individual *is* qualified. Since my focus was so narrow, once I realized there was no fit for various people I met, those interviews were concluded fairly quickly. I did try to be nice about it, but why continue for any great length of time when the outcome was already obvious?

After a couple of years I came to the realization that I was looking at the interviews in the wrong way. Granted, a particular candidate might not be right for a particular situation, but I wasn't learning much about that person. I was not considering the types of positions where he or she might really fit. Perhaps in the near future I might get another assignment where these people's experience and qualities would be perfect.

So I started looking for the good points in every potential candidate, took notes, and kept them on file for future possibilities. It also allowed me, on occasion, to make helpful suggestions to them in terms of their career growth. Most important, it established positive relationships that with many were the beginning of long-term friendships.

You may have neighbors or coworkers who for one reason or another tend to turn you off so you avoid them as much as possible. Perhaps you make quick judgments about people based on very limited information that really doesn't allow for a qualified judgment. Or perhaps you have people working for you that you don't consider promotable even though you have spent little time with them. If so, your attitude is much like mine used to be, and you are missing out on some valuable opportunities. A winning attitude does not make snap judgments. Go out of your way to get to know more about people and look for the good in them. In most cases you will find it, and it will enrich your life as well as theirs.

A friend of mine became vice president of operations for a multiple-factory manufacturing company a few years ago, and he told me that during his first few months he became concerned with the high trucking costs involved in receiving raw materials and in shipping finished goods at one of his factories. The factory manager couldn't answer his questions about those costs and shifted the blame to the traffic manager, suggesting that the man was probably getting too old to handle his job.

My friend sought out the traffic manager, finding him in a small, almost-hidden-away office. In less than two hours he knew he had uncovered a gem. The traffic manager knew the problems and knew the solutions, but his authority had been undermined and his suggestions ignored. My friend changed all of that. After uncovering a number of other problems in the way that factory was being managed, he replaced the factory manager and made sure that the traffic manager had the necessary authority.

"Cost came back in line so fast I couldn't believe it." My friend laughed. "After a few months I gave that traffic manager responsibility over the traffic departments in the other two factories as well. He is now sixty-three years old and is known as the Silver Fox of our industry." He grinned as he added, "I also made sure that he got the raises and the bonuses he deserved."

An attitude that is outgoing and includes looking for the good in people will bear fruit in your career and in leading a more fulfilling life.

A Confident Style

Just about any child can learn to ride a bicycle. The amount of time it takes, however, is dependent on his or her confidence level. Usually Dad starts by pushing the bicycle. When he gets up to speed, he lets go and says, "Pedal!" Until the child's confidence level reaches a certain point, instead of pedaling faster when that front wheel starts to wobble, the child hesitates—and down she goes.

Success in any endeavor is very much affected by the level of confidence we exhibit in approaching that endeavor. Confidence in ourselves and our ability to do something greatly increases the odds that we will successfully complete the task in front of us.

Experience is an important factor in an attitude that exhibits confidence. If we have successfully handled some particular task before, it is relatively easy to be confident that we can do it again. As we gain experience, however, we want to bring that same confident attitude to new, unexplored areas. People who lack confidence don't like to try new things. They are hesitant about taking on new responsibilities, and their very lack of confidence is often what is holding them back in their career growth.

There is a danger, of course, in being overconfident. This can lead us into situations we can't handle, resulting in failure and perhaps setbacks in our careers. We have to learn our limitations. But I have known a lot of people who have settled for less than their talents could have gained for them. In just about every case, it was caused by lack of confidence in themselves.

This confidence factor in our attitude is linked closely to the positive thinking factor we considered earlier. We might think of confidence in terms of putting into action the positive thoughts we apply in looking at problems and opportunities. Our positive attitude says it can be done, and we then apply the confidence factor when we do it. Successful accomplishments will generally result. If they don't, find out what went wrong, learn from the experience, and try again. We don't want to lose confidence in ourselves just because once in a while we don't get it right.

In just about anything we do, the level of our self-confidence will have a major influence on the results. It will also play a role in whether we live a hesitating, up-and-down life, or one characterized by steady progress and measurable accomplishments.

A Humble Spirit

This is an often overlooked factor in a correct or winning attitude. If people have an upbeat, positive, confident, and outgoing attitude, they generally find themselves moving ahead in their careers and making accomplishments. As a result, they are quite pleased with their progress.

The problem that can easily develop is the growth of pride and smugness. It can become "my" accomplishments, "my" possessions, and "my" victories. The ego inflates, and suddenly arrogance is added to our overall attitude, and perhaps even a touch of disdain and contempt for those with lesser talents.

What is it that we are that we haven't been given? We can use our talents to their fullest, but we were given them to start with. Are we taller or better looking from our own efforts? We have to exercise to be strong, but did we provide the body that exists that lets us be stronger than others?

Each of us starts out with what God has given us—our body, our looks, and our talent. Certainly we can have a sense of satisfaction if we make the most of what we were given, but truly great men and women recognize that what they are was given to them by God.

A humble attitude is simply one that gives the glory to God in victories and looks to God for help in defeat. It neither gloats over winning nor despairs over losing.

Humility is the factor that keeps our feet planted solidly on the ground and allows us to lead a balanced life where people will like and respect us for the way we live our lives, rather than for what we have.

A Winning Game

Those of you who play golf are aware of the annual "Skins" game that is televised. This competition brings together four of the top professional golfers of the year. The game in 1996 consisted of Tom Watson, Fred Couples, John Daly, and the newest star of the tour, Tiger Woods.

The format is eighteen holes of match play—which means that each hole is a contest unto itself. The golfer with the lowest score wins the hole and the money allotted to it, but if two players tie for low, the money carries over to the next hole. The first six holes are worth $20,000 each. On the second six the ante goes up to $30,000, and the last six are worth an impressive $40,000 each.

As the game progressed, the importance of attitude stood out in stark contrast between two of the players—John Daly and Fred Couples.

Tom Watson was probably the most consistent of the four, and he won the most money of the first nine. Twenty-year-old Tiger Woods was playing in this format for the first time, and although he ended up in third place with only one "skin," he played well and gave the viewers the idea that he would be back even stronger next time.

The more interesting duo, however, was John and Fred.

Both were having difficulty getting putts to drop. Daly kept pushing his to the right, and his frustration was evident. He showed signs of anger and, after the second or third time he let a "skin" elude him, his loss of confidence became evident and his attitude appeared negative. You could see it in his posture and in the almost careless way he addressed the ball and got his shots off quickly.

Couples, on the other hand, kept smiling and maintained his composure despite his own problems.

Somewhere around the fifteenth hole, Daly had a short putt that was worth $200,000. As he lined it up, he just couldn't seem to get his self-confidence back. It came as no surprise that the ball slid past the hole by two feet.

Two holes later, Couples was in the same situation, but because of carryovers the hole was worth $280,000. He lined the putt up and set himself in the same way he always did. He approached that putt with the same positive and confident attitude that characterizes his game, and it gave him the plus he needed. The putt went in, and Fred won the competition in a very similar manner to the way he had won it the year before.

Maintaining a winning attitude is difficult, if not impossible, to do all of the time. Our emotions are too strong for that. The death of a loved one, for example, will hardly allow us to be upbeat when we are first grieving. Difficulties with children, the loss of a job, or any other serious adversity can temporarily result in negative thoughts and disrupt a positive and confident outlook.

Our emotions will affect us, but, since we know that, we simply have to face the reality that we will have our down times. It may take a little time to return to the frame of mind that we want, and we have to use our willpower to gradually get those emotions back under control. In those instances we can turn to God even more fervently, and he will help us through. He will never leave us. In him we will find the comfort and grace we need to get our lives back on the right track and to move ahead again with a "winning" attitude.

You'll notice we're at the end of this section and we've only mentioned five of the six secrets of success:

1. Live in the now, not the later
2. Define your goals
3. Pay the price
4. Discover the law of reciprocity
5. Develop a winning attitude

There is a sixth secret to come, but we're going to save it for the end. First, we need to look at six obstacles to success—those roadblocks that life throws at us to keep us from reaching our full potential.

2
Obstacles to
SUCCESS

Self-Pity: Admitting Defeat

$\int$uppose we were attending a track meet. In the infield, we can see the runners preparing for the fifteen-hundred-meter race. We see eight contestants nearing the starting line. They are wearing racing shorts and lightweight shirts and the best track shoes Nike or Reebok can make. They have trained hard for this race, pushing themselves to peak physical condition, which will allow them to maximize their running ability. The eight lanes are clearly defined by white lines running around the track.

Now, suppose that this is an unusual track meet. Before the race begins, the runners pick up a variety of obstacles and place them in various positions down the lanes. Some obstacles are fairly small, requiring only a break in stride to get over, while others are larger, greatly increasing the time and effort needed to get past them. A couple of the runners put up obstacles so high that it's questionable whether they will actually be able to clear them at all.

The eighth runner, however, has only a few obstacles in his lane. In fact, the obstacles are so small that it's obvious that he will not be hampered to any great degree. Now, this particular runner may or may not have as much natural ability as the other seven, but as we look at the track, it soon becomes apparent that he will win the race, simply because the others have handicapped themselves to the point where they will have little chance of winning. Some might not even finish the race! Watching from the stands, we wonder why they were so foolish as to put obstacles in their own paths.

That is exactly what many people do all the time in their lives. In fact, we've all done that at one time or another. Whatever our role in life, we are running with different obstacles in our paths. The great tragedy is that, just like the runners, we actually put those obstacles there ourselves.

These obstacles may appear to come from outside ourselves, but we are the ones who embrace them and even let them grow larger until, eventually, we can find ourselves stumbling over them every day.

In doing so, we find ourselves unable to meet our goals or to perform at levels our talent should have brought us to. When this happens, we can become frustrated and discouraged. Because these obstacles have become such a normal part of our lives, we may not even recognize how much they handicap our performance or the control they exert over us. That's why I refer to them as stumbling blocks to success.

We are going to consider some of the most common stumbling blocks. They will all be familiar, and I suspect that every one of us has encountered them from time to time. Some of us may be dealing with them effectively—not letting them take root or getting rid of them when they do show up.

For many others of us, however, these stumbling blocks may be causing great difficulty because they have become deeply embedded in our lives. The good news is that we don't have to let them keep growing. We can cut them down in size, deal with them effectively, and, in many cases, get rid of them completely.

The first step is recognizing them and considering what roles they are playing in our lives. We also have to make the conscious decision that we *want* to get rid of them. In spite of their insidious characteristics, however, they can get so inter-woven into our thoughts and habits that the decision is not as easy as you might think. Simply knowing something is bad for us may not be enough to push us into a commitment to stop do-ing it.

Six Obstacles to Success

There probably are an unlimited number of things that can get in between you and the successful achievement of any goal. But I'd like to consider six such obstacles that I believe to be the most common roadblocks most of us face on our path to suc-cess.

These are self-pity, poor self-image, guilt, fear, bitterness, and adversity.

There are several characteristics of stumbling blocks that we need to keep in mind as we examine each more closely.

For one thing, while stumbling blocks may hinder our prog-ress, it's important to realize that the process of dealing with them actually helps us to grow. By overcoming a stumbling block, we get stronger. We develop the skills to tackle other stumbling blocks, and we grow in both personal and spiritual ways.

Stumbling blocks tend to trigger our emotions. We get up-set, frustrated, angry. But if we let our emotions rule our lives, we will be on a roller coaster of ups and downs that will leave us drained and exhausted. Knowing that stumbling blocks are emotionally charged ought to compel us to approach them dif-ferently—using our will rather than our emotions.

Another characteristic of stumbling blocks is that when we accept them, allow them to hinder us, we only hurt ourselves. They waste our time, eat at us, prevent positive action, divert our attention from using our talents, and lead us astray from the paths we are trying to follow. Some of them can even de-stroy our physical and mental health.

Perhaps the most significant characteristic these stumbling blocks share is their ability to limit or even prevent us from reaping the benefits of successful living—namely, peace of mind, happiness, and contentment. We'll take a closer look at each one and see how we might take steps to minimize or eliminate its effects, starting with that classic time-waster, self-pity.

Admitting Defeat through Self-Pity

Some of the stumbling blocks are easier to deal with than others, and self-pity is perhaps the easiest. It is such a waste of time that a little common sense dictates our dropping it as soon as it appears.

Unfortunately, times when we can feel pity for ourselves appear very frequently. Why is it that it rains one hour after we washed the car? Why does our lane of traffic sit still while the others move on their way? Why is our flight canceled when we get to the airport? Why does our baggage get lost? Why does our elevator stop at every floor?

The list—like life—can go on and on. A toothache always occurs at an inappropriate time and, of course, we always catch a cold just as we are about to go on vacation. These are just common situations, but it's easy to let self-focus give us the idea that bad things happen only to us.

Usually self-pity is a much bigger hindrance to our success than the obstacle that triggered it. Self-pity immobilizes us; it's a form of admitting defeat. We feel sorry for ourselves, back away from the obstacle, and become discouraged from pursuing our goal.

Someone once said that of all the traps and pitfalls of life, self-pity is the deadliest, "for it is a pit designed and dug by our own hands, summed up by the phrase, 'It's no use—I can't do it.'"

One of the steps we can take to rid ourselves of self-pity is to look objectively at people around us. Almost all of us can think of other people with more difficulties than we have. If we are objective, then we know that when it rains, it rains on other people too. We are not the only ones caught in traffic jams or stuck in elevators. When things are beyond our control, there is simply nothing to be gained by fretting about it and feeling sorry for ourselves. Instead of wallowing in self-pity and wasting time, we should take a number of positive approaches to help us move on with life.

First of all, we can avoid situations that frustrate us and let self-pity in the door. If traffic jams and slow elevators are a problem, we should plan our time better. Have you ever noticed how all the lights seem to turn green when you're not in a hurry?

We can also recognize that self-pity is not only an emotional reaction, but it's actually rooted in pride. We think this is "our time," "our plan," and "our schedule" that is being disrupted, and our self-importance that has been deflated. Some reflection on our part to see things objectively and not subjectively will go a long way in getting rid of self-pity.

A sense of humor also helps. It's amazing what laughing at ourselves once in a while will do to put self-pity in its place.

Finally, we can also make good use of the time we have been wasting. Let's assume we are caught in a traffic jam. Rather than turn to self-pity, we can listen to some good music or commentary on Christian radio, or we can listen to an educational, motivational, or uplifting Christian book on tape.

Better yet, we can talk to God. If we want a void to be filled, he is the one who can do it. Besides, consider how often and how much time we *could* have spent with him when we were wasting those periods on self-pity. And maybe communing with God will become a habit—one we will never want to break if it becomes ingrained. (Incidentally, when we are talking with him, we don't have to babble on. He already knows our problems. It is really more rewarding to listen from time to time.)

We should realize that other people, even though they may

also grovel in self-pity from time to time, really don't like it when they see it in *us*. They back away and interpret it as whining, which can quickly cause them to lose respect for us and avoid us. We don't need self-pity, and we don't have to have it in our lives. If we recognize self-pity for what it is, we can stamp it out every time.

About two years ago, a very good friend of mine, who happens to live a few houses away, became senior vice president of stores for a large retail chain. It was an excellent move for him careerwise, but had the disadvantage that the location of the home office of the company made it necessary for him to drive about sixty-five miles each morning and evening.

His company is more than willing to relocate him, but that has several drawbacks. Their friends and their children's friends are all in the area where they currently live. The children are involved in a lot of activities that they really don't want to change. His wife is willing to move if that's what he wants, but he knows that she would prefer to stay where they are.

In any event, Cary decided he could handle the travel. But he admits to a certain amount of self-pity at first. "It really seemed to waste a lot of time every day," he told me.

After a couple of months of growing frustration, he decided to see if he could change a disadvantage into an advantage. His first step was to leave earlier in the morning. Doing that eliminated a lot of the traffic problems he had been encountering and actually reduced his travel time by fifteen to twenty minutes every morning. It also permitted him to work out at the company's fitness facility before work, and before long he started trimming down and feeling better. In addition, he was able to be at his desk earlier, giving him a head start on the day.

Second, he began using the driving time in the morning and evening to listen to a broad variety of Christian tapes, including readings from the Bible. Then he bought a set of teaching tapes so that he could learn Spanish.

"The self-pity disappeared pretty fast," he told me with a smile. "I really feel better. I dropped fifteen pounds, and Spanish is not as hard as I thought. Best of all," he added, "that time with God is the most rewarding part of my day. Even if we do move closer to work someday, I'm not going to give up all the positive values I've gained from something I once thought was wasted time. The real waste was my self-pity."

Cary's actions illustrate a good point. When self-pity shows up, look for a silver lining in whatever is causing it. You may well find that you can turn a disadvantage into a plus and derive some unexpected and rewarding results.

Poor Self-Image: Selling God Short

If you listen carefully when you interact with other people, you'll be surprised at the number of self-critical remarks you hear. "I didn't do this very well," or "I wouldn't be good at that if I tried," or "I really messed up on that report."

If you listen closely, you may be surprised to hear how often you say the same sort of thing. You might hear how you would like to be taller or shorter or slimmer, or how you are concerned about losing your hair, or how you wish you were more outgoing.

It's important to have a humble spirit about ourselves, of course, but self-deprecating talk doesn't achieve humility, only self-doubt. What we forget is that others tend to look at us based on our own evaluation of ourselves. What we are actually doing is calling our perceived faults or shortcomings to their attention.

Low self-esteem is a problem we all face from time to time. Usually it is short-lived and we have the resources to pull ourselves out of it. But sometimes there is a darker side to poor self-image that can go far beyond limiting the effective use of our talents and result in much more serious problems.

The Danger of a Poor Self-Image

In the late 1970s my wife and I, along with our son Bob, flew to Hawaii for a combined business and vacation trip. One afternoon when we were on the beach, Bob was swimming and I noticed a young couple sunning themselves nearby. I was struck with the beauty of the girl's face, but when she stood up to put on some suntan lotion, I saw that she was almost unbelievably thin. Martha was also shocked and commented that she looked like she had been in a concentration camp.

A little while later Bob returned. As he noticed the couple, he whispered to us, "Do you know who that girl and fellow are? They're the Carpenters."

I looked again, and indeed it was the singing duo that was so popular at the time—Karen and her brother, Richard. At that time it would have been difficult not to be familiar with their music. Turn on a radio program that played recorded music, and before long you would inevitably hear Karen's beautiful voice. She and her brother were rapidly becoming superstars in the field of popular music.

Karen was the epitome of wholesomeness in the early 70s and was welcomed by a public tired of Vietnam and antiwar protests. The Carpenters' rise to fame was rapid.

We know now the story that was beginning to be played out during our brief encounter with them on the beach that day.

The pressure of stardom conflicted with a serene life, and Karen started to feel lost and out of control. Her self-image was low, and it took a beating from the constant attention from the press. Having a journalist call her plump in print was perhaps the final straw, and she took control over the one thing left in her power—food. She put herself on a strict diet of salad and iced tea.

Her continuing weight loss did not affect her singing, but when she collapsed on stage during a performance, her problem became public. She went to New York for medical help, but career pressures quickly mounted, and Richard was impatient to get back to work. Karen soon pronounced herself cured, and everyone was all too willing to believe her.

She returned to a whirlwind of appearances, but still with a poor self-image and a shaky ego. In desperation, the young woman from Downey, California, found solace in vomiting and taking laxatives. In February 1983, at the age of thirty-three, Karen was found dead in her bathroom. The cause was diagnosed as a heart attack stemming from complications from anorexia and bulimia.

Overcoming Low Self-Esteem

Karen Carpenter's is not an isolated case. There are over 2 million American men and women, usually between the ages of fifteen and thirty-five, who suffer from anorexia, bulimia, and other eating disorders.

But low self-esteem can lead to other problems as well—drug use, alcoholism, pornography, and other addictions. A person doesn't have to come to the tragic extremes that Karen Carpenter did in order to be plagued by these signposts of a self-esteem problem. Many lives are hindered from real success because of secret addictions.

A key step in overcoming low self-esteem is understanding how we are deceived by it. In order for it to take hold, we have to accept someone else's standard for a good self-image. In other words, what we do is measure ourselves, whether it be in terms of appearance, talent, or even worth, and apply it against what we have been led to believe is acceptable. Then many of us mentally nod our head and agree that we are somehow lacking.

This can start in our early years when parents, perhaps inadvertently, compare us with our siblings or other children. For teenagers, being "accepted" is all-important, and when we see others who are more popular, better students, better athletes, or better looking, we begin to doubt ourselves. Hollywood and Madison Avenue reinforce those feelings of inferiority.

As we get older, this tendency to compare ourselves to those who move ahead more easily causes our view of ourselves to become increasingly negative. With this type of attitude, we can become more tentative, less willing to compete, and we avoid being center stage whenever possible. As a result, we may miss opportunities because we believe we won't measure up even if we try.

Once again, we can see the "self-focus" that is a characteristic of all the stumbling blocks. In this instance, our self-focus is negative in nature. Rather than looking positively at our strengths, we let our perceived weaknesses rule our thoughts and, subsequently, our actions. Self-deprecation takes over in our attitude and our words. Many of us go through our entire lives this way, never making the most of what we have, deceived into thinking that we will always have to settle for less than what we really want.

The real problem of low self-esteem, of course, is that it sells God short. He created us. He made us unique individuals with certain characteristics, abilities, and talents. Low self-esteem is telling God that he didn't do a good enough job in creating us. When we do that we are focusing on the negative—what he *didn't* give us—instead of focusing on the positive, being grateful for what he *did* give us.

Fortunately, it is never too late to change. It does require a change of attitude, however, and a realization that we don't have to compare ourselves with *anyone*. We have to develop the determination that we will focus outward rather than inward. And we have to learn to trust in God's wisdom in making us who we are.

Perhaps the first thing many of us have to deal with is physical appearance, which is basically unimportant. Many people who are leading successful lives are not tall, dark, and handsome or slim, blonde, and petite. They accept themselves as they are and make the most of the talents they possess. They work hard, are kind, and love their spouse and children.

Acceptance of ourselves should not be determined by the

people who, in the opinion of mainstream media or Hollywood movie producers, exemplify what we are supposed to look like or be like. In fact, as we look around objectively, we will see that most of the people we know don't meet those false criteria any more than we do. If we can stop calling our self-perceived problems to their attention, we will find that others will accept us just the way we are.

Low self-esteem can lead us into allowing the physical side of our lives to dominate the spiritual side. As we do, we reduce our focus on God and our capability to love others. This can only diminish the intimacy of our relationship with them. If it continues over a period of time, our poor self-image will continue to grow.

Redirect Your Focus

We have to turn from a focus on "self" to looking outward to others. Being concerned for others gets us away from the focus on our self-image. When we look for the good in others, we will find it. When we show interest and love for others, we will find it reciprocated.

The adage that "love conquers all" is true. It may be difficult at times, because other people also have poor self-image and may not immediately respond. But over a period of time, a caring and loving person will generally find that same concern and love being reciprocated. If our hearts are filled with love, no room is left for a poor self-image. It's that simple.

Guilt: Plagued by the Past

We feel guilty about something when we have a sense of responsibility or accountability about something that we failed to live up to. If you and I agreed that I'd call you on a certain date, and I didn't, then I would likely feel guilty later on. My guilt would leave me feeling bad, and I'd apologize to you for letting you down.

Guilt is connected to these two important concepts—responsibility and forgiveness.

These days, guilt has gotten a bad name. People think that because guilt leaves them feeling bad, they need to get rid of it. To eliminate guilt from their lives, they get rid of their responsibility—the "shoulds" of life—that they fail to live up to. The argument is that the effects of guilt are far more destructive than the effects of irresponsible living. As guilt is eliminated and responsibility is relinquished, forgiveness becomes a lost concept.

The irony here is that only those people who truly have a sense of right and wrong are those who experience guilt, along with responsibility and forgiveness. Those who live irresponsibly don't have to endure the feelings of guilt in their lives

This doesn't seem just or fair or right, of course, and it is perplexing—until we discover a very important thing: There are two kinds of guilt—good guilt and bad guilt.

Good Guilt and Bad Guilt

If we do something wrong—such as taking advantage of or hurting someone else—our conscience is alerted and we become aware of our fault. The feeling of guilt is the red flag, the sounding of an alarm that calls for us to correct the situation. For many of us, that is just what we do. We acknowledge our fault to God and take the necessary steps to correct the situation.

This is good guilt—part of God's system of grace that is based on a motivating sense of responsibility and morality, followed by forgiveness and love. As God does with us, so should we do with others.

So how can guilt be such a problem? First, we may not take the steps we just mentioned. Initially, we may try to rationalize the situation, since being totally honest with ourselves is not the easiest thing in the world. Pride comes into play, and it's human nature to avoid admitting we are wrong.

While we rationalize a situation, we often delay taking corrective action. The sense of guilt may abate, but generally it returns, stronger and more insistent. We are playing a dangerous game when we rationalize our actions. It's entirely possible that we may successfully rationalize our action and bury the guilt far beneath a layer of pride.

It becomes easier to bury guilt a second and a third time, and it's not too long before we can do it on bigger things. This process hardens our hearts and allows pride to rule our lives. Left unchecked, this pride will eventually cut us away from the love of family and friends.

When we bury guilt deeper and deeper inside us, it becomes "bad guilt"—bad in the sense of the absolutely destructive power it wields in our lives.

Sins of the Past

Sometimes it's impossible to ask forgiveness of someone for reasons beyond our control. Perhaps the person or persons involved in the situation have died, or perhaps they are far out of our sphere of influence. In other words, we may literally not be able to do anything about it. In this type of situation, many people have to live with a guilty conscience—a conscience that detracts from every pleasurable achievement.

For Christians, this need not be a problem. When we acknowledge our guilt to God, we know by his Word that we are forgiven (1 John 1:9). If we cannot get to a person we have wronged (or if we can and the person rebuffs us), we have no further guilt. The matter is in God's hands, and he will take care of it.

Yet feelings of guilt may continue to bother many people. The reason for this is our inability or unwillingness to forgive ourselves. Even when we ask God to forgive us, a sense of unworthiness and continuing guilt suggests that we doubt whether forgiveness has actually been given.

This presents a problem for a lot of us—a sad problem. For one thing, it directly interferes with our relationship with God. Despite the clarity of Scripture, which tells us that Jesus paid the price for our sins and that if we acknowledge our faults he is quick to forgive, we harbor doubts that he really means it. Instead, we bring up the old problems each time we approach him in prayer or meditation.

Think, for a moment, about a little boy and his father. The boy, who has been disobedient, admits his wrong and asks his father to forgive him. The father may scold or punish him, but afterward he takes the child into his arms and forgives him for whatever wrong was committed.

Suppose, however, that every time the little boy approaches his father, he starts apologizing all over again. By bringing up the past, he is holding back and missing opportunities for a loving relationship. The father wants to give love, but his love goes unrequited.

This is, in effect, what we do when we continue to carry

around guilt for our sins—sins that we have already acknowledged to God and that exist only in our mind and emotions. God *knows* our weaknesses and our faults, but despite our imperfections, he still loves us.

He also wants our love and thankfulness for what he has done for us. When we can't forgive ourselves, we are not only denying his Word, we are limiting our ability to receive the blessings he wants to shower on us. By blocking off our fellowship with him, we refuse happiness and peace of mind. We allow the stumbling block of guilt to control us.

J. B. Phillips, a canon of the Anglican Church, wrote a number of books before his death in 1982, including *Your God Is Too Small.* That book examines the diverse ways people think of God. Phillips showed many examples—some humorous—of how a human being's concept of God will inevitably fall short of his true glory.

The reason, of course, is that we can only draw upon our human experiences. No matter how we expand and elevate those experiences, we cannot truly conceive the reality of a limitless God. That's one reason why many Christians have an inability to understand the depth of God's love when it comes to guilt.

In our own experience, most of us can forgive someone who offends us. Depending on our nature, we may forgive that person a number of times for the same transgression. There comes a point, however, when we really don't want to be around that person if he or she continues to commit the same offense over and over. Under those circumstances, the relationship is, at best, strained.

If we think about God and his forgiveness in human terms, there is a nagging thought that if we keep repeating a particular sin over and over, then at some point God will want no part of us. This kind of thinking plagues people who are carrying around guilt and feelings of unworthiness.

Jack Hayford, well-known Christian teacher, author, and pastor of the Church On The Way in Van Nuys, California, spoke on this subject one day on his radio program.

"Suppose I had committed a particular sin 292 times in the past, and then do it again," began Dr. Hayford. "How can God think I am sincere when I have sinned again and again and then repented and asked for forgiveness again and again, and yet I have done the same thing another time? I am ashamed and don't even feel right in approaching him. I delay for a while, but finally I face up to my sin and say to God in sorrow, 'I did it again.' Do you know what God would respond? He would ask, 'You did what again?'"

Pastor Hayford was making the point that sins of the past are just that—sins of the past. They were forgiven by God and placed as far away from us "as the east is from the west" (Psalm 103:12). When we repent, regardless of the number of times we may have committed that same sin in the past and received forgiveness for it, it's as if we have committed that sin for the first time.

We can't limit God or his unconditional love. Our God is bigger in every way than we can possibly conceive. Guilt is our problem, not God's. Jesus took care of sin and guilt once and for all. We have to trust in him and his Word. This is the way to drive this stumbling block out of our lives forever.

OBSTACLE #4

Fear: Paralyzed
by the Future

When we talk about fear, we have to include its sibling: anxiety. Fear and anxiety are among the most serious stumbling blocks to successful living. Their negative influence not only inhibits the use of our talents, which limits our achievements, but it can also rob us of all joy in life itself.

Anxiety has a way of feeding on itself, and it can grow to the point that it not only diminishes our performance but also endangers our health. As anxiety grows into fear, it can eat away at us to such extremes that it can actually prevent us from functioning at all. Anxiety and fear are among the most difficult stumbling blocks to stamp out of our lives.

Concern, Anxiety, and Fear

The first positive step we can take is to distinguish between concern and anxiety. There is a tremendous difference between them. *Concern* is a normal reaction to a situation affecting us adversely. Having a toothache or a nagging cold are proper matters for concern. If we receive a poor work evaluation or if we sense some dissatisfaction from our superiors, we would be less than human if we didn't react with concern. *Anxiety,* on the other hand, is worrying and fretting about matters that should only concern us. If we start doing that, our imagination can

83

take over, and we easily move from a "now" focus to an unknown future filled with negative possibilities. Instead of facing up to situations, evaluating their impact, and doing our best to correct them, we let anxiety in the door.

As anxieties grow in us, their manifestations have a way of transmitting themselves to other people who, inevitably, will react negatively. Ironically, by letting anxiety show, we can bring about the very things we fear the most.

Getting rid of anxiety is not easy. Doctors can prescribe tranquilizers, but drugs, of course, just treat the symptoms rather than getting to the root causes, and sometimes they can lead to secret addictions.

An effective way of dealing with anxiety is to talk out our problems with our spouse or close friends. They can help us see our problems objectively, which allows us to develop plans to overcome them.

The very best way to get rid of anxiety, however, is to turn to God. He is always there to help, and we can always trust and rely on him. His Word assures us that he will never desert us.

Fear, an extended form of anxiety, is a major problem for many people. Fear is being paralyzed by the future. It's a common malady in this day and age. As William Lyon Phelps said years ago, "The fear of life is the favorite disease of the twentieth century."

Like some of the other stumbling blocks, fear does have a good side. If someone threatens our safety, for example, the adrenaline flows and we are better prepared to handle the situation. In most cases, the initial reaction of fear stimulates our body's senses.

The problem is that our body can't tell the difference between real and imagined dangers, so it reacts the same either way. If anxieties about ongoing situations build up into unending fear in our mind, they can create a bondage that disables us from taking any action at all.

We can see evidence of people with these bondages all the time. For example, we all know people who are afraid to fly, afraid to be home alone, afraid to drive, or afraid to ride elevators. Fear in many different forms can work its way into our lives.

Dealing with fear head-on is a daunting task. In many cases, people will simply avoid fearful situations. They won't fly, or they won't drive or use elevators. They will do everything in their power to avoid disturbing situations.

Of course, this sidetracks us from the path to success. We deal with fear by avoiding different chunks of life, and in doing so, we cannot achieve the goals before us.

Overcoming the Fear of the Future

Ultimately, there is only one effective answer to this obstacle of fear and anxiety: God himself.

Over and over in the New Testament we find the words "Do not be afraid." We are clearly told that God has not given us a spirit of fear, but rather a spirit of power, love, and discipline (2 Timothy 1:7). Virtually every epistle starts with a blessing like this one from Galatians: "Grace to you and peace from God our Father, and the Lord Jesus Christ" (Galatians 1:3). In the Old Testament, we find the same call to place our reliance on God. David declares in Psalm 23, "Even though I walk through the valley of the shadow of death, I fear no evil; for Thou art with me; Thy rod and Thy staff, they comfort me" (Psalm 23:4). And in Psalm 56 he asks, "In God I have put my trust; I shall not be afraid. What can mere man do to me?" (Psalm 56:4). This call to trust in the Lord is repeated again and again.

One of the key things we must do is logically think through what is so frightening to us. If we fear a person or a situation, we can take steps to avoid or neutralize the particular person or situation.

One of our deep-seated fears—one that has been with us since the days of Adam—is the fear of dying. When a plane suddenly lurches and our stomachs turn over, our reactions are rooted in the fear of death.

Now we know in our heart of hearts that death is inevitable. What should concern us more is what happens *after* death. For Christians, the answer is clear and comforting. Whether death comes knocking at an advanced age, or whether death results from an unexpected accident or illness, dying is simply a doorway to an eternal life with God.

This is what we should have deep in our hearts: the knowledge that, in accepting Jesus as Lord, we have also accepted God's gift of salvation and that we will spend eternity with him in heaven.

In today's world, there will always be dangers lurking about—dangers that raise feelings of fear inside us. While prudent behavior can minimize our risks, we know that any precautions we might take still have limitations. As Christians, we must put our faith in God, knowing that his power, compassion, and unconditional love will sustain us in any situation.

During his lifetime C. S. Lewis was a popular lecturer at Oxford and a renowned professor of medieval and renaissance literature at Cambridge. He also became a successful and widely read author. Interest in him was renewed in America when, in 1995, he was portrayed by Anthony Hopkins in the hit movie *Shadowlands*.

One of the most popular and widely read of his more than thirty books was his classic *The Screwtape Letters*. The book has an interesting format, consisting of a series of letters from a senior devil to a junior devil who is on his first assignment, which was to lead a human away from God and heaven. Lewis's idea was to present the psychology of temptation from the other point of view.

In one chapter, questions about anxiety and fear are examined to show why the powers of wickedness want humans to think in terms of the future rather than the present.

In this letter the senior devil points out that the present is the only point that touches eternity. It is only in the "now" that humans have an experience analogous to the experience that God has of reality as a whole. God wants us to be concerned with that present—either meditating on our eternal union with him or obeying the present voice of conscience, bearing the present cross, receiving the present grace, and giving thanks for the present pleasure.

Satan wants us living in the future, which is completely unknown to us. There are two reasons for this. First because it interferes with receiving grace, which only can be provided in the "now" of our lives; and second because, being unknown, it leads us into living anxious and fearful lives. He wants a whole race perpetually in pursuit of the imagined treasure at the rainbow's end. He wants us never honest, never kind or happy "now," and missing out on every real gift offered to us in the present.

When we reflect on it, we can see that our anxieties and fears dwell in a future that doesn't even exist until it becomes "now." Being fearful about the outcome of an operation that may become necessary, or living in a constant state of anxiety over job security can keep us from experiencing the love, peace, and grace that is only offered to us in the "now."

We want to keep our focus in the present, with the full knowledge that Jesus is with us and remembering his promise that he will never leave us. Inevitably, we will encounter problems, but rather than letting anxiety and fear lead us into living in anticipation of them, we must trust the God who loves us to be our daily strength. We can be totally confident that he will see us through any situation.

In Jesus Christ, we conquer the future and overcome fear in our lives. As the psalmist says: "The Lord is my light and my salvation; whom shall I fear? The Lord is the defense of my life; whom shall I dread?" (Psalm 27:1).

Bitterness:
The Cancer Within

Bitterness encompasses a group of feelings and behaviors, including bigotry, cynicism, hatred, jealousy, and revenge. All of these ingredients can come to a boil and drive out love—leaving us, in the end, separated in spirit from our fellowman. No matter what we achieve in life, when love is gone, we are left only with bitterness. This stumbling block can be the most destructive one.

Each member of this family of obstacles is rooted in two common tendencies. One is our inclination to judge people; the other is to let our "self-focus" enter into our personal relationships and various situations of our lives.

To see how these negative forces can develop and grow within us, we should first understand the difference between "not liking" and "disliking" someone or something.

Not liking is passive. When we were children, most of us didn't like certain foods. We may have eaten spinach because our mothers insisted it was good for us, but when we were older, we never touched it again. It's the same with people. Some folks we instinctively don't like. It's nothing personal, but we may not be attracted to them, so we try to minimize our contact with them.

Dislike, on the other hand, requires a more active evaluation. We have to consciously make a judgment to dislike someone or something, and sometimes that decision is based on relatively little information. We make judgments about people—usually based on first impressions—and from that point, we think about them in a negative way. We look for opportunities to deride or demean them, which becomes a self-fulfilling prophecy to support our views.

The next step is to build this stumbling block higher and broader. In other words, we transfer our dislike from one person to a group of people. We judge them without even knowing them. As we do so, our dislike and mistrust fester like an open sore. The result is bigotry, whether it is referring to African-Americans, Caucasians, Asians, or certain religious groups. Rather than seeing people as individuals, we view them through the prism of hatred. We attribute the characteristics of one to many, which can expand our dislike to a whole grouping of people whose only similarity may be their particular color, religious beliefs, or ethnic origin.

When bigotry takes root, the next development is cynicism. We gradually view all people with a sense of mistrust, and we are not surprised by any sort of negative actions on the part of anyone. We become cynical about people, and we expect the worst. As these feelings grow day by day, our love of neighbor has no room to thrive.

Rather than looking for the good in people, we search for the bad. In the process, we fail to notice that love is leaving us. Our relationships with others, even those close to us, become cool and reserved. We are separating ourselves from others without even knowing it.

If these feelings continue to grow, we will have no one left to share our dreams, successes, failures, joys, or sorrows. We will have driven people away and eliminated any support system. As we grow further away, we are more and more alone; contentment has been replaced by bitterness. We may try to im-

press people with our accomplishments or our worldly possessions, but our lack of love is reciprocated. That's when we
finally realize that there is no real feeling of affection or love
being returned.

Hatred is a long way down a road that started with dislike.
Hatred can appear when there is an action on the part of someone that affects us personally and usually in a serious way. Perhaps it stems from someone cheating or taking advantage of us,
or hurting us in one way or another. Whatever it is, we take
each insult personally, resenting it deeply.

Hatred only heightens the damage we cause ourselves when
we give in to the forces of dislike, bigotry, and cynicism. Hatred
detracts from the productive use of our talents. It consumes our
thoughts as we dwell on ways to get even, to get revenge. The
saddest part is that revenge is such an empty cup. Even if we get
our pound of flesh, revenge provides only a fleeting moment of
satisfaction. With revenge, there can be no long-term satisfaction, no joy or happiness.

Overcoming the Malignancy of Bitterness

The ironic thing about this family of obstacles is that when one
of them takes root in us, we may feel as if we are getting back at
others. In fact, we are only hurting ourselves. Bitterness, anger,
and hatred grow inside us like a cancer, and eventually they
hurt us more than anyone else.

Certainly success cannot grow in a life of bitterness and hatred. It is the cancer that grows instead, feeding off of everything else that is good and right.

It was Harry Emerson Fosdick who quipped that "hating
people is like burning down your own house to get rid of a rat."

Overcoming these bondages starts with recognizing that
these stumbling blocks are clearly forms of self-destruction.
We think we are hurting other people by disliking or hating
them. Instead, we only hurt ourselves. If we allow love to de-

part from our lives, we are dooming ourselves to a bitter and lonely life.

It is so easy to see the faults of others and to rationalize our own. We tend to judge others by their actions and ourselves by our motives. Under this guise, we can criticize people because we want to help them do better, but if they criticize us we resent it. We can drive our cars recklessly and jump lanes because we are in a hurry, but if others do the same, we react in anger.

Just as fear is the opposite of faith, hatred is the opposite of love. Inherent in hatred is unforgiveness. If God can love all people and, particularly, if he can love us, we should come to the realization that love is what it is all about. It's not always easy, but we have to work at it.

As we demonstrate love, we will find it reciprocated. If we stop judging others, we will also find ourselves not being judged. When we turn away from self-focus and look for the good in people around us, we will make startling discoveries about others and will reap the rewards that true fellowship brings.

As Christians, we should meditate on the reality that God has forgiven us; despite all of our faults and failures, he loves us. Again and again in Scripture Jesus commands us to love one another. If he can forgive us, then it can only be pride that is holding us back from forgiving our neighbors.

There will be some people, of course, with whom we will have trouble making headway. That should not upset us, however, nor should it diminish our willingness to meet them more than halfway. What we don't want is any hatred in our lives to cause the loss of love in our hearts.

A Forgiving Spirit

The real fruits of success are found in a loving heart. A story from my own experience illustrates the power of a changed heart in overcoming not only bitterness, but guilt as well.

Some years ago, I interviewed a man named Phil for a senior sales position in the consumer packaged goods industry. He had a fine background of education and experience and impressed me as being well qualified for the position.

The only questionable area was a one-year stay with another company six years earlier. He had turned down a relocation offer and chose to leave the company and change jobs instead. This decision temporarily set back his career, but he had progressed well since that time.

When I asked Phil to expand on the situation six years ago, he explained that a change in top management was the key factor in his decision not to relocate. Family considerations also played a role, plus the fact that the new location was less desirable. Reference checks supported his statements. At that point, my only concern was a sense of bitterness he betrayed whenever we discussed that particular situation.

In the end, Phil was highly regarded by my client and was selected for the new position. We had a number of meetings during the interview process, and we developed a friendship after he assumed his role in the new company. Some months later, Phil asked me about my reference checks at the company where he had been six years earlier.

"Did you check with their senior vice president?" he asked as we ate lunch one afternoon.

"I've known George a number of years," I told him, "and I did talk briefly with him. As you know, Phil, he had joined the company himself only a month or two before you left. He checked the records, called me back, and gave me the names of a couple of executives who knew you better. They all gave good references."

Phil laughed, but not with humor.

"I doubt that he had to check the records. He was the cause of my leaving and all my resulting problems, which lasted for more than two years until I worked my way back up."

I was surprised at the anger and bitterness in Phil's voice. "I don't understand," I said.

"George came into the top sales job from a big competitor," Phil stated. "It was a tough period economically, but my area was doing well. I only met him once to say hello, and then the next thing I heard was that he was bringing in some of his own key people. I was offered the option of a transfer and a relocation to a smaller region down South, or I could just get out. It was that simple."

Phil thought for a minute, then continued. "Now we are direct competitors," he said, "and, if I can, I'm going to run right over him."

Phil wasn't kidding. I could *feel* the depth of his feelings. His face had tightened, his mouth turned down. I saw a man who felt he had been wronged. He had obviously been brooding about it and was now going to even the score. What I was seeing was not attractive, and I was concerned for him.

We met again later that week, and I brought up the subject again. We talked first of Phil's perception of the situation. Based on the limited facts available to him, he had jumped to conclusions that may or may not have been true. Most important, he saw the evidence only in terms of himself—how each factor affected him and his family. No consideration had ever been given to his former company or to George himself.

Phil grudgingly admitted that there might be some truth to my observations. "But the way it went down is just too obvious to me," he said.

I changed course. "Tell me, Phil, does holding a grudge have any effect on George? According to you, he met you only once and got rid of you quickly. How has your unforgiveness hurt him in the last six years?"

Phil looked off in the distance, then turned to me. "Well, I guess it hasn't hurt him, but if I take away enough of his business, it will affect him then."

"OK," I continued, "let me ask you a more important question. How has the unforgiveness of the last six years affected *you?* What have *you* gotten out of it?"

This question startled him and caused him to think. He stared at me for a long time, and then he suddenly rose and walked out. He didn't say a word. He just stood up and walked out of the restaurant. My spirits sank. *I really blew it,* I thought.

Two days later, Phil called me and asked if he could drop into my office. When he arrived, he was calm but subdued.

First, he apologized for walking out on me. "It was the question," he explained. "That question has hit me a hundred times in six years, but I've never answered it. I keep ignoring it again and again."

He got up and walked over to a window. "I've really thought about it these past two days, and I think I can answer it now."

"What did you get out of it?" I began.

"Nothing really," he replied. "Less than nothing, in fact, because of the negative feelings I have lived with over the years. I've experienced bitterness, anger, and even hatred sometimes. I can't really believe the hours I've wasted on it. Plotting revenge has had other effects, too. My wife has been upset over it, and she's told me a hundred times to give it up. She's even told me I should pray about it, but somehow . . . well, I haven't, and I just sort of ignore the situation when I do pray."

He paused and then added, "I know it's not right, but I was really hurt, and I wanted to get even."

We discussed the matter for a while longer, and then I suggested that he meet George face-to-face.

"Actually, he is a nice guy," I told him. "I really think it's important that you face up to this, Phil. It's tearing you up inside, and you know, deep down, that unforgiveness, bitterness, and hatred runs against the grain of what you know is right."

It was tough for Phil to admit it, but he nodded slowly. "I know," he said softly. "I know."

Even in that first step of awareness, I could see the beginnings of relief and hope stir within him. Phil didn't want to make a direct call, so he asked me to set up the meeting.

I was a little surprised when I called George. I expected him not to pick up on Phil's name at first, but he knew it immediately. Then he sounded hesitant and asked about the purpose of the meeting.

"What does Phil want?" he asked. "Is he looking for a job?"

The questions jumped out, but I reassured George that Phil was just a former employee who had felt wronged, and he simply wanted to clear up some feelings that had been bothering him. George finally agreed to meet him in two days.

A week later, I heard from a different Phil. He was relaxed, relieved, and happy, but it went deeper than that. Phil had been through a life-changing experience, with results beyond anything he could have imagined.

"We actually had two meetings," Phil told me to my surprise. "Frankly, the first one was tough. I went to his office, and he was pretty reserved and very suspicious. I told him my version of the facts and how I had reacted when the change in management had occurred. He told me that you had called, and he checked the records. But he said he really didn't remember the incident since it was over six years ago," said Phil.

"Actually, I hadn't reported directly to George when he came on board," Phil continued, "and he told me that he really had very little to do with the decision to offer me a relocation package. Well, I felt pretty awkward, but I faced up to it and told him how I had blamed and resented him all these years.

"George seemed to warm up a bit at that point, and he asked me a lot of questions about how leaving the company had affected my wife and kids. I was candid with him. I told him I had had a rough time, and the cut in pay cost my family a nice house and canceled a lot of plans we had made. Anyway, I finally asked him to forgive me. He seemed embarrassed and kind of brushed it off, telling me to forget it. Then the meeting was over."

"But you mentioned two meetings," I said.

Phil grinned. "Yeah, there was another one. First of all, though, I can't tell you how good I felt after seeing George the first time. The relief was unbelievable. It was as though iron clamps had been removed. My wife was happy, too.

"That night I prayed again, and my wife and I prayed together. It really meant a lot to us both, and I want to thank you again for our talk two weeks ago."

"The other meeting," I said impatiently. "Tell me about the other meeting."

"Well, George called me the next day and asked me if he could come over to my office. When he arrived, he was in a nervous state—I mean he was really upset. He closed the door and looked me in the eye. Then he finally said, 'I lied.'

"I was a bit stunned, and I told him I didn't understand. George then repeated his statement. 'I lied,' he said. 'I remembered you very well. I got rid of you because I was insecure and scared. Getting that new job six years ago was a big deal for me. I felt I had to have people I knew and trusted to be successful in my new assignment. During the first year I got rid of five or six people and brought in my own team. You were just one of the first to go.'

"Then I told him, 'Hey, that's all right. A lot of people feel that way when they take on a new job.'

"But then George interrupted me. He said, 'I know, but I can't excuse myself that way. I was scared. I didn't give you or your family or any other family one moment's consideration. It is one thing to replace a position, but it is something else when my motives were self-oriented.'"

Phil paused and looked at me. "It was quite an experience," he said. "Up to that point, I had only felt my own resentment, my own unforgiveness. Then I realized that George had been all bound up with his own problem of guilt. I had only wanted to get even, and there I was consoling him and forgiving him."

Then Phil smiled, "I guess I did get even. He forgave me, and I forgave him."

Life goes on, but Phil is a happier man. He has encountered problems since that episode, but unforgiveness is not one of them. George is also a happier man. He told me that he had been in contact with the other people he had replaced. They were all very nice about it, and each accepted his apology, except for one who wouldn't speak to him. George felt badly about that, but he hasn't let it detract from the new freedom he has found.

"Guilt was robbing me of every joy of accomplishment," George confided, "and it was growing—not diminishing."

Later that evening I thought about what might have happened. Phil could have refused to see George and let his bondage increase, continuing to plot revenge and missing out on joy and peace of mind. Or, Phil could have seen George but been rebuffed by him and had his apology refused.

In that event, Phil would still be free. He didn't actually *have* to have George's forgiveness. He had done his part, and in doing so, he had turned to a far greater power for the healing that he had been refusing for many years.

As for George, he might have gone on being consumed by guilt and robbed of the pleasure of each accomplishment. Or, suppose Phil and the others rebuffed him by refusing his apology and still hated him? That wouldn't affect George at all, because he, too, had a greater friend to wash away the guilt.

Phil and George had each slipped into a bondage of their own making. By freeing themselves, they rediscovered the joy God provides for those who believe in him and walk in his will.

Adversity: You Aren't in Control

No matter how well organized we are or how well we prepare for contingencies, we will face adversity in our lives. In fact, in terms of certainty, adversity ranks right up there with death and taxes. As Paul Harvey has said, "In times like these, it helps to recall that there have always been times like these."

Life is a continual process of change. That much we can count on. After we are born, we continue to grow and mature physically, mentally, and emotionally. We work, marry, have children, buy homes, change jobs, relocate, and, we hope, retire one day. We make friends, but then we move on and make new ones. It's impossible to maintain the "status quo" for any prolonged period.

A major factor in this change process—a catalyst for change—is adversity. By definition, it connotes a "going against"—usually referring to our own interests.

Adversity, of course, appears in numerous forms, and it can range from minor inconveniences to major traumatic experiences. Regardless of its impact, however, adversity pulls us up short in whatever we are doing or in whatever direction we are going at the time. The initial reactions can range from annoyance to dismay or even panic.

Fortunately, however, we can find a bright side. In fact, if we keep adversity in the right perspective, we can deal with it rather effectively. We can not only minimize its negative aspects, but we can even reap beneficial results and personal growth from it.

Before discussing this perspective further, we should recognize two important facts. The first is that when we come to grips with adversity, it is a battle with no neutral ground. Depending on our attitude and our actions, we will emerge from the skirmish either stronger or weaker.

The reason for this is that once adversity strikes, the process of change is immediately in effect. We either fight to control that process (and fighting itself can be a strengthening action), or we let adversity control us, which leaves us in a weaker condition for the next time, when it can strike again.

The second fact is that despite its inevitability, we can take some steps to minimize its impact. Prudence in financial matters, for example, minimizes money problems. A regular savings program builds financial resources for those "rainy days" that crop up from time to time. What we eat and how much we exercise influences our health and longevity.

The old adages "An ounce of prevention is worth a pound of cure" and "Look before you leap" suggest that prudence goes a long way toward minimizing the common forms of adversity. For most of us, however, prudence is not a long suit, meaning that we usually learn by experience, much in the same way that young children learn to leave a hot oven alone by touching one.

Despite our best efforts, however, there is no way we can completely steer clear of adversity. Fortunately, we don't have to just surrender to it. Once it has intruded into our lives, we can take a number of steps to deal with it effectively. Let's walk through them together.

Face It

While this may seem fairly obvious, the fact is that many of us don't face adversity head-on. Instead, we try to ignore it or rationalize it away.

A sad case in point is people who ignore symptoms of illness, thereby setting the stage for more serious health problems later. Similarly, in the business world there are usually symptoms before more serious aspects of adversity become evident. For instance, the attitudes of superiors and peers generally start to change negatively for a period of time before we're passed over for promotions or even lose our jobs. During performance reviews, we might hear suggestions about improving our attitude or performance relative to our interpersonal skills.

While these are minor adversities in themselves, if we fail to face them and take them seriously, they can often lead to far more disagreeable consequences. Thus, the earlier we sense adversity, the more quickly we can deal with smaller problems before they escalate.

Learn from It

It is vital that we understand that adversity is a teacher. An achievement may be pleasant, but in the giddiness of the moment, we tend not to learn very much from it. Adversity, on the other hand, can teach us many things—if we're willing to learn from it.

Someone has said, "In this life we will encounter hurts and trials that we will not be able to change; we are just going to have to allow them to change us."

The first thing we can discover is where we had been putting our focus and to what degree we value certain people or things. When adversity strikes, its impact is directly related to how much we value that person or thing. For example, let's say we hear of a car accident involving an acquaintance down the hall. That news will generally have less impact than an accident involving a close friend.

A financial reversal might have little impact on people to whom money is not of critical importance, but it can be devastating to those whose primary focus is accumulating as much money as possible. Even a traffic jam can prompt great frustration and emotional distress to those who've placed *their* time and *their* schedule at the forefront of priorities.

Aside from where we've placed our focus, another lesson to learn from adversity relates to the "how it came about" question. In some situations, it may be a tough break—just one of those things. Many times, however, we will discover that we actually brought the adversity on ourselves.

That's because the law of reciprocity is always operating, but the willingness and the ability to recognize and accept this is not easy. It involves analyzing situations objectively and looking at them in an open, honest manner. Pride steps in and tries to block this step. Unfortunately, if we fail to learn the lessons that adversity teaches us, then we are setting ourselves up for similar things to happen over and over again.

As I've reviewed the business careers of men and women over the years, I've been astonished to see the cyclical patterns emerging in people's résumés. Many individuals seem totally unaware of the patterns or their own role in them. When I ask questions, as I did of Phil, they will comment on personality clashes or differences in management styles as they explain numerous job changes. "It was office politics," they will say. I hear that a lot.

Any one of those could be a valid reason for changing jobs, but when it occurs again and again, it suggests to me that some deeper consideration must be given so that a true understanding of what happened and where the fault lies can be gained.

We need to learn from adversity and discover where it is we have our true priorities, in order to keep from repeating our failures and becoming derailed from the tracks toward true success.

Share It

When adversity strikes, there is a tendency to withdraw from others. It is much easier and more effective, however, to share with others. This, in itself, can be another learning experience, since we will discover fairly quickly who really cares and who doesn't.

In a world where the pursuit of money and the things money can buy take a high priority, it should come as no surprise that adversity is perceived as a menacing enemy to be avoided at all costs. Not only is it to be shunned, but we also learn that when it strikes us, a lot of people start avoiding us as well.

Despite this reaction, however, there are many people who do care and will offer to help during trying situations. Adversity can be a shocking, numbing, and hurting event, but this is a time for a family to stand together and grow stronger as a unit. Sincere friends who've gone through major periods of adversity can offer significant help in minimizing and overcoming its impact.

Look for Opportunity

Although adversity has an initial negative impact, it almost always carries a positive factor, and that is called opportunity. As we have seen, adversity creates a "change" situation, which means we are presented with alternatives. When this occurs, we should look for the silver lining—the opportunity to turn the situation around to our benefit.

Many of us, for example, are in jobs we really don't like. We feel somewhat trapped, but inertia and routine—plus a mortgage—keep us plugging away. We may feel that we are not getting anywhere, but since the bills are being paid, we just hang in there. Losing a job changes all that, but in the long run the effect may not be negative.

Why is that? Suddenly, we are free to make some choices. What kind of work do we really like to do? What are we best at? Where would we like to live? Generally, severance pay is connected with a termination, which provides some time to consider possibilities.

Again and again over the years, I have talked with people who, in looking back, will identify serious adversity as a time when changes were forced upon them but recognize those changes ultimately led to more productive and financially attractive career growth.

This "opportunity" aspect of adversity is not limited to business careers. It occurs in every aspect of our lives—an illness, a loss of a friendship, anything at all. If we face adversity squarely, we can learn that opportunities will present themselves in ways we might not have suspected.

Consider some of the people for whom adversity has yielded great opportunities and successes:

- John Bunyan wrote *Pilgrim's Progress* while confined to a prison cell for his views on religion.
- Henry Ford failed and went broke five times before experiencing success.
- Winston Churchill was beset with personal failures and severe depression before rising to the challenge of leading the free world through the ordeal of World War II.
- Actor James Earl Jones overcame a severe stuttering problem as a child. Today he is known for the richness and power of his voice.

Adversity will come your way at some point in your life—you can be sure of it. The question is how you will deal with it and use the opportunity it gives you.

Act on It

The final step in dealing effectively with adversity concerns action. When we face adversity, we can sense and see an opportunity to learn from it. Unless we act, however, we are still being controlled by change instead of taking charge of the situation.

Initially, taking action requires that we exercise our will rather than letting our emotions take over. A natural first reaction to adversity is shock. We experience a time of inaction that can easily lead to self-pity. We feel guilty. Our self-image is affected. We lay the blame on someone else, and suddenly we're tripping all over the stumbling blocks to success.

To overcome this, we must take the emotion out of it, and we must use our willpower to think objectively. Then, as we implement the principles for setting and attaining goals, we develop a course of action. When an opportunity presents itself, we should seize upon it and act. As we take steps of action, we know there will be new challenges, new situations, and perhaps new adversities. The more effectively we deal with each one, however, the stronger we will be to handle the next one.

We can't always exert much control over the onset of adversity in our lives, but we can control how we look at it and the choices we make on how we handle it. We can fight back, stand our ground, and plan our next move. By seizing these opportunities that adversity provides, we can turn defeat into victory and allow growth in our lives.

It was J. C. Penney who said, when asked the secret of his success, "Adversity. I would never have amounted to anything had I not been forced to come up the hard way."

How God Uses Adversity

There is another side to all of this, of course. It's important that we recognize and consider the spiritual component of adversity. It would be nice if God shielded us from adversity so we could just cruise through life without concern.

As a matter of fact, that is precisely what happened in the Garden of Eden when God created Adam and Eve. When evil entered the world, however, everything changed. Now we live in an imperfect world, where disease and illness and physical death are unavoidable. Yet, God gave us a free will to make choices in our thoughts and actions.

We can choose to keep those thoughts and actions in line with God's Word, or we can yield to the temptations from the forces of evil. These temptations are around us all of the time, and we are all vulnerable on occasion. When we yield, the consequences can be devastating.

Many people tend to think of God's commandments in a negative sense. The "thou shall not" parts suggest to some that God intends to limit our enjoyment of life. The reality is exactly the opposite.

What good can come out of things like theft, covetousness, adultery, or murder? The damage we do to others and ourselves is obvious. God gave us the Ten Commandments as a guide for successful living. When I say guide, I do not mean that they were simply suggestions. God wants us to walk in his will, and if we do so, we will be under his protection and can receive his blessings.

We recognize that all of us will face different adversities from time to time. They can appear through no fault of our own, and they certainly can appear through the choices other people make. From a Christian point of view, however, it's clear that stepping out of God's will opens the door to adversity. This is not a choice we want to make lightly.

From a spiritual point of view, the steps to coping with adversity are essentially the same as from the physical viewpoint—but with one important plus. We know we must face adversity and recognize it for what it is. If we have yielded to evil by stepping out of God's will, we know we have a forgiving Father who has provided us with an easy way to step back under his protection.

The big plus is that regardless of how other people react to our adversity, we can share it with God. He is a powerful ally to have. We have a God who "causes all things to work together for good to those who love God, to those who are called according to His purpose" (Romans 8:28). He can open our eyes to the opportunities that adversity presents, and he can influence and bring those opportunities to us. We must put our faith and trust in him—not in circumstances.

Nothing in Scripture suggests that we will go through life without adversity. All too often, people tend to blame God when things go wrong, instead of looking to him for the solution. We have the assurance that God will see us through it.

Remember, adversity is a learning experience. It's an opportunity to grow closer to God and to grow spiritually.

Turning to God when adversity strikes is the surest way to cope with it effectively.

Ask God for Help

Now that we have discussed the various "stumbling blocks" to success and have seen the need for God's help in all areas of our lives, we are ready to look at the sixth secret to success and successful living.

I believe it is the most important one.

As humans, we all have limitations. Most of us recognize this, and when we run into situations we can't handle we look around for help. We go to doctors when we are ill and to dentists when we have toothaches. We procure the services of skilled tradesmen to make repairs that we are unable to handle ourselves. If we need money for a new house or car we often turn to a lending institution to help us in closing the transaction.

It makes sense to turn to people who have the necessary knowledge, skills, or financial resources when we have problems that they can help us solve. But what about problems that are more complex and, for any number of reasons, help may not be so readily available? Suppose our illness doesn't respond to the prescribed medicine or we can't get in contact with a doctor. What do we do when love is going out of our marriage or we have a spouse who is cheating? Suppose we have a child who is going down the wrong path, experimenting with alcohol and drugs? Where do we turn when we find ourselves in a rut as far as our career is concerned or have difficulties in effectively using our talents? Suppose a business venture is turning sour and we are looking at bankruptcy?

The list of potential problems could go on and on. When we looked at the first five secrets of success, we considered practical guidelines to make the most effective use of our talents and to progress more rapidly in our careers. Despite our best efforts, however, we may still sense that the use of our talents is limited.

Fortunately, there is another way to enhance our own efforts. We can turn to God and ask for his help. He has no limitations. He loves us and cares for us, and, if we read Scripture, we know by his Word that he wants us to turn to him for the help we need. I don't know who coined the phrase "God helps those who help themselves," but it would seem more appropriate to say, "God helps those who need help and who turn to him and ask for it."

If we turn to Scripture we find the words of Jesus on this subject in the Gospel of Matthew:

> Ask, and it shall be given to you; seek, and you shall find; knock, and it shall be opened to you. For everyone who asks receives, and he who seeks finds, and to him who knocks it shall be opened. (Matthew 7:7-8)

In the next three verses, Jesus also makes clear that he is not simply referring to major needs but to our daily needs, large or small.

> What man is there among you, when his son shall ask him for a loaf, will give him a stone? Or if he shall ask for a fish, he will not give him a snake, will he? If you then, being evil, know how to give good gifts to your children, how much more shall your Father who is in heaven give what is good to those who ask Him! (Matthew 7:9-11)

Over the years I have discussed those passages with many people, and there were those who immediately protested. They said they had asked but didn't receive. Some would also state that they knew lots of people who had problems and their requests were also to no avail.

This subject of asking and receiving is a difficult one. God is always true and faithful to his Word, but his thoughts are far beyond our comprehension, and he takes into account factors we can't possibly know. We might think, for example, that coming into a lot of money would resolve all of our problems. But God knows us intimately—our strengths and our weaknesses. He also knows the future. He may see that a lot of money could actually be a curse for us, leading us away from him. We might not have the ability to handle a lot of money wisely, perhaps making risky investments and ending up worse than before. We also don't know God's timing. We may be asking for something we want right now, while in God's all-knowing perspective it may not be the right time, or perhaps he has something better that he will provide at a later time.

Another reason we may not receive the answers we desire is because of obstacles to receiving God's help that we may have set up in our lives. These obstacles can prevent or limit the responses that we would like to receive. Before we consider them, however, let us look at the importance of asking for help in the spiritual side of our lives.

In Paul's letter to the Ephesians we read:

> For our struggle is not against flesh and blood, but against the rulers, against the powers, against the world forces of this darkness, against the spiritual forces of wickedness in the heavenly places. (Ephesians 6:12)

We know that temptations are all around us, and Paul is telling us that our battle is against Satan and the spiritual forces of wickedness that are trying to lead us into yielding to those temptations. Because of our human weaknesses, it is a battle we will lose if we rely only on ourselves. While God's help in the practical side of our lives provides us with opportunities, his help in our spiritual life is an absolute necessity.

We are no match for Satan if we try to stand alone. The good news, however, is that Satan is, in turn, no match for God. In God we have an all-powerful ally. Jesus overcame Satan at the Cross, and when we accept him as our Lord and Savior we can turn to him when temptations appear. We can have complete confidence that he will provide us with the help we need to overcome them. In his first letter to the Corinthians, Paul tells us

> No temptation has overtaken you but such as is common to man; and God is faithful, who will not allow you to be tempted beyond what you are able, but with the temptation will provide the way of escape also, that you may be able to endure it.
> (1 Corinthians 10:13)

The help God provides is his grace. His grace contains the spiritual life, love, and power we need. Grace is such an important subject that we will consider it again later in this chapter and in more detail in the final chapter of the book, where we will present a Christian perspective on success.

For now we will turn back to the practical side of our lives to review the obstacles that may be interfering with receiving the help God can provide us. We have already alluded to the first one.

Ask for Help

There are a number of reasons why many people don't ask God for help in their day-to-day activities. While they generally will turn to him in serious situations, such as a critically ill child or if they have to undergo major surgery themselves, they may not ask for help in the smaller problems they encounter each day. It's as if they think God is too busy or perhaps doesn't have an interest in the more mundane demands of the particular career path that they are following.

I have a friend who owns a restaurant in a large southeastern city. He mentioned one day his concerns because business had fallen off, but when I suggested we pray about it he seemed almost shocked. *Why would God be interested in the restaurant business?* was his attitude. "God is too busy to worry about my little problems," he said. "I'll get by."

The reality however is that God *is* interested in everything we do. Think back on those Scriptures in the Gospel of Matthew that we considered earlier. The examples of a "loaf" and a "fish" were not huge, significant items. These examples make it clear that God does want us to turn to him to ask for his help in small matters as well and to trust and rely on him to meet our needs. He is never too busy to hear us. My restaurant friend is simply missing out on opportunities for help by putting limitations on the limitless God.

Another reason many people don't ask for help is found in the compartmentalizing of their lives that we mentioned earlier. God time is fine for Sundays; but when it comes to work it's back to "business is business," and self-reliance comes to the forefront. Despite the problems, the worry, and the setbacks, they go it alone and miss out on getting God's help in solving daily problems.

Caught up in the pressure and tempo of a typical business day, I often find myself doing the same thing. Even though each morning I ask God to help me and to direct my footsteps that day, it is very easy for me to forget about him as the day proceeds. Usually—and particularly when things start falling apart—I catch myself and sheepishly turn back to him for help. It is astonishing sometimes how rapidly the problems are sorted out, fall into place, and solutions appear.

You probably have seen those television ads where, after talking about the qualities of his product, the salesman looks into the camera and says with great sincerity, "I guarantee it." I generally do not find this very convincing. As we read Scripture, however, we see that when we ask God for help, it is God who guarantees he will answer. We have his word on it. I find *that* very convincing.

Don't Take Problems Back

I suspect we all have a tendency to do this on occasion. We have problems that are causing us worry and stress, and we take them to God to tell him about them and ask for his help. Then as we get into bed and pull up the covers, we take them back, try to come up with solutions, and find ourselves worrying again and losing sleep.

In her book *The Christian's Secret to a Happy Life*, Hannah Smith illustrates this point with a story about an elderly woman walking down the road with a large, heavy load on her back. A man on a horse-driven cart pulls up beside her and offers a ride. She gets in, heavy load and all. The driver suggests she put it in the back of the cart, but she tells him that she doesn't want to be any more of a bother to him. As they ride on she still is carrying that heavy load.

I think we all have the tendency to do the same thing. It's somewhat like an Oprah talk show. People come in to air their problems, and there is a lot of talk back and forth. But when they finally leave, they generally take the same problems right back with them.

When we give our problems to God, we need to leave them with him. He is far more capable of handling them than we are. We don't know his timing, but we have to trust and rely on him. If those problems pop up in our mind again and we find ourselves fretting and worrying, we need to quickly give them back to him. We don't want self-reliance to take over in place of trusting in God. This doesn't mean that we don't do our work, but it allows us to do it more effectively, and it opens us up for the very help we have requested. Trusting God to enlighten our minds and show us the answers is a great way to reduce stress.

Have the Right Motives

We should always think about our motives when we ask for God's help. Are our desires actually rooted in pride? Are we asking for things to show off how successful we are or to take pleasure in the envy of others? Is money becoming an idol in our lives, and are we actually asking God to give us more so we can build that idol bigger?

The Epistle of James was written to Christian Jews who were scattered geographically. James takes them to task about this question of motivation:

> What is the source of quarrels and conflicts among you? Is not the source your pleasures that wage war in your members? You lust and do not have; so you commit murder. And you are envious and cannot obtain; so you fight and quarrel. You do not have because you do not ask. You ask and do not receive, because you ask with wrong motives, so that you may spend it on your pleasures. (James 4:1-3)

We have a loving and generous Father, but he will not answer prayers that are simply rooted in pride or that will lead us away from him.

Does this mean that we shouldn't be asking for help in using our talents more effectively and in career advancement, both of which carry with them the likelihood of increasing our incomes? Not at all. There is nothing wrong with the desire to provide good educations for our children or to enjoy a nice home, cars, and other conveniences that make life more enjoyable for ourselves and our families.

We have a generous God who has given us talents and who will help us use them effectively. But there are conditions.

At one point in Scripture, Jesus is talking with a crowd of people who are concerned and anxious about their physical needs. The response of Jesus is found in Matthew 6:32-33, where once again the conditions relative to God's promises are shown. After assuring them that God knows their needs, he says: "But seek first His kingdom and His righteousness; and all these things shall be added to you."

When we keep God first in our lives, we will have the right motives when seeking his help.

Eliminate Doubts

This is a very serious obstacle for some people. I don't believe in the "name it and claim it" attitude I have heard some people express, but it is important to trust God and to rely on him to do what is best for us. In the same letter mentioned earlier, James addresses this issue:

> But if any of you lacks wisdom, let him ask of God, who gives to all men generously and without reproach, and it will be given to him. But let him ask in faith without any doubting, for the one who doubts is like the surf of the sea driven and tossed by the wind. For let not that man expect that he will receive anything from the Lord. (James 1:5-7)

Most of us have a tendency to let doubts creep into our minds after we have asked for help. We may even be asking in a doubting way. We ask, but we have negative thoughts about God's willingness to provide the needed help. This attitude goes against God's Word. Repeatedly we are told to ask with confidence.

When we ask God for help, we know he is faithful to his word, and we can be confident that he hears us and will respond in our best interests.

Get Rid of Unforgiveness

As we discussed in an earlier chapter, bitterness and unforgiveness are key obstacles to successful living. It comes as no surprise, then, that these negative traits are another major obstacle in getting help for our problems.

Forgiveness is an inherent characteristic of God. When we repent of our sins, he is quick to forgive them. He also wants us to love one another and to forgive others when they wrong us. This subject is mentioned frequently in Scripture. In Matthew 6:9-13, Jesus is telling us how to pray and gives us the Lord's Prayer, or the "Our Father," as we sometimes refer to it. Verse 12 says: "And forgive us our debts, as we also have forgiven our debtors."

In Paul's letter to the Ephesians we read: "Be kind to one another, tender-hearted, forgiving each other, just as God in Christ also has forgiven you" (Ephesians 4:32).

In the Gospel of Matthew, Peter asks Jesus how many times he should forgive a man who sins against him. He asks if he should forgive seven times, and Jesus answers, "I do not say to you, up to seven times, but up to seventy times seven" (Matthew 18:21-22). The phrase *seventy times seven* suggests an infinite number.

Forgiving is not always easy. An abused or sexually molested child can be affected very deeply and carry bitterness and unforgiveness well into adulthood, or even for an entire lifetime. There are many very serious wrongs that can leave deep scars.

If we keep that unforgiveness in our hearts, however, we are clearly going against God's will and have established a major obstacle to receiving God's help. On the other side of the coin, we can bring that very obstacle to him and ask for his help to get rid of it. For many people it is really the only way they will get rid of it.

Some people are able to just block the offending person out

of their mind, but that is not forgiveness. In Matthew 5:23-24, Jesus indicates how important it is to reconcile past problems when approaching God: "If therefore you are presenting your offering at the altar, and there remember that your brother has something against you, leave your offering there before the altar, and go your way; first be reconciled to your brother, and then come and present your offering."

We know that God forgives us our sins if we repent and ask for forgiveness. We should also remember, however, that he will also forgive the very person we can't forgive if that person also repents and asks for forgiveness. If we ask him, he will rid us of this problem and let us see the situation concerning us in a new way that will allow us to have the peace of mind we really want.

Clear the Pipeline to God

As we read Scripture, it becomes clear that God wants us to get rid of the obstacles we have just reviewed. It may be easier to do that if we understand exactly why he wants us to eliminate them.

All God's help to us, including our salvation, are gifts from him that come to us by his grace. He created us with free will, however, so we make the choices. We can accept or reject his gifts.

When we accept Jesus as our Lord and Savior, a personal relationship is established that allows us to have fellowship with God the Father. The nature of that relationship is pivotal to leading a successful life, and we will consider it in more detail in the last chapter.

For now, though, we should realize that God's grace comes to us through Jesus. In human terms we might think of it as a clear pipeline that has been connected to us through which the grace flows. When we are in close fellowship with God, the pipe is open and grace flows easily. If we put obstacles in the pipe we are limiting that flow. The point is that we are not limiting God from offering us grace, rather we are limiting our ability to receive it.

In Psalm 37:4 we read: "Delight yourself in the Lord; and He will give you the desires of your heart."

Can you see from this passage the intimacy of the personal fellowship God offers to us? The obstacles we have reviewed interfere with that fellowship. We don't ask for help, we doubt he will grant us our requests, we take our problems back after asking for help, we have the wrong motives, or we may be unforgiving of others. Can you see how these are plugging up the pipe and interfering with or limiting that flow of grace?

We must always realize that if we get rid of those obstacles that limit the flow of God's grace, we open ourselves up to the gifts he offers us each day. And if we ask him for help, he will give it.

We have a God who answers prayer. Just ask him.

3
Ultimate
SUCCESS

The Friend

And behold, a certain lawyer stood up and put Him
to the test. . . . Wishing to justify himself, he said to
Jesus, "And who is my neighbor?"

Jesus replied and said, "A certain man was going
down from Jerusalem to Jericho; and he fell among
robbers, and they stripped him and beat him, and
went off leaving him half dead. And by chance a certain priest was going down on that road, and when he
saw him, he passed by on the other side. And likewise
a Levite also, when he came to the place and saw him,
passed by on the other side. But a certain Samaritan,
who was on a journey, came upon him; and when he
saw him, he felt compassion, and came to him, and
bandaged up his wounds, pouring oil and wine on
them; and he put him on his own beast, and brought
him to an inn, and took care of him. And on the next
day he took out two denarii and gave them to the
innkeeper and said, 'Take care of him; and whatever
more you spend, when I return, I will repay you.'"

Tom Perrelli had been out of work for three months, and the
father of two was starting to panic. Armed only with a high

school education and a fierce determination to succeed, he had worked his way up from laborer to supervisor to foreman at a textile mill.

After twenty-three years with the mill, he had been recently promoted to superintendent. Warehousing and distribution were his areas of responsibility, and he was well liked and respected by his colleagues at work, as well as by the customers and the trucking firms he dealt with.

Then Tom's plant was acquired by a large eastern company, and the consolidation of operations that decimated the smaller company came with startling rapidity. Just four months after the announcement of the change in ownership, Tom received a curt letter terminating his employment and outlining his final benefits. He never met the man who fired him.

The economic impact of his dismissal was cushioned somewhat by a termination package, which included his unused vacation time. He also had a small savings plan with the company, but there was no retirement program or other benefits. With a son entering his senior year in college and a daughter only a year away from high school graduation, Tom's cost of living required a fairly good income. Thus, losing his job came as quite a shock. However, at the age of forty-two, Tom was confident he would find another position easily. As it turned out, he was wrong.

The first few weeks of his job search went by rapidly, as Tom responded to advertisements in the business section of the newspaper. He lived in the suburbs of a good-sized city, and the job-market section was several pages long. He learned very quickly, however, that relatively few positions were applicable to his work experience. For the few that were, he mailed out letters and résumés.

The results were minimal. In most cases, he heard nothing, and the rest of his letters prompted little more than an acknowledgment of receiving his job application.

During that same period, Tom called a few friends and suppliers of his former company to see if they had anything available. While most business friends expressed sympathy, the conversations were short and fruitless.

One Sunday afternoon, Tom dropped by and visited his pastor. It turned out to be a bad time, because the meeting was interrupted by several phone calls. Finally, the pastor had to excuse himself for an appointment that had been previously scheduled. Other than gentle words of encouragement, the pastor offered no solid advice or help.

One evening Tom's wife, Ann, suggested that he call John Grant. Tom hesitated. John Grant was an elder at their church whom they had known for many years. Though they didn't know each other socially, they were well acquainted from various church functions. Mr. Grant was president of a successful business in town, and Tom wondered if he might have an opening. He really did need a job, so after more discussions with Ann, he made the call.

Later that evening, John mentioned to his wife, Laura, that Tom had called about a job. "You know him from church, Laura. His name is Tom Perrelli. I think his wife's name is Ann."

"Yes, I remember them," Laura said. "You're not going to hire him, are you?"

John looked up. "Why not? I think we have some sort of need in our shipping and receiving area. I was going to check it out in the morning."

"Whatever you think is best, dear," Laura replied. "I thought we agreed that you were going to keep church and work separate, though. I mean, you do have people from the plant here socially from time to time. Really, I'm not sure how they would fit in."

John was tired. "Well, I hadn't even thought about it that way. You're probably right. Business is good, and I'm sure Tom will find something pretty quickly." He reached for a second helping of roast beef and promptly forgot about Tom Perrelli.

The next six weeks were a trying period for Tom and Ann. Although they tried to shield their children from their concerns, Tom was getting more nervous and upset. He had not applied for unemployment benefits, both from a sense of pride and a conviction that he would find a new job fairly quickly. Now he was beginning to question that decision.

Tom didn't know where to turn. He had registered with a number of employment agencies, and while a few had called back, the opportunities had been ill-fitting. More important, the pay offers were almost 50 percent lower than his last position. As he and Ann got on their knees each evening, their prayers took on a more fervent and desperate tone.

It was at this low point that Tom received a telephone call from Jerry Carson. Jerry had been the personnel director at Tom's former company, and he, too, had lost his job following the takeover. Since their interaction was infrequent, Tom remembered him vaguely as a young and pleasant man, but that was about all.

"I saw you in town last week," Jerry said, "but I didn't have a chance to say hello. Have you found another job yet?"

"No," Tom replied. "I have looked at a few things, but—well—nothing has developed yet."

They talked a few minutes about Jerry's new company. He had found an excellent position with a large company downtown. For a few moments, Tom thought hopefully that Jerry might have an opening.

That hope was dashed when Jerry stated that the company had put a temporary freeze on new hires. "That should change in a few months, though. Maybe we will have something then."

Tom's spirits sank. *In a few months,* he thought, *I'll be bankrupt.* He thought Jerry was going to hang up, but instead he continued.

"The main reason I called is . . . well, as you know, I'm in personnel, and we do a lot of interviewing, hiring, things like that. I was thinking that you probably have never had to look for a job before, and I wondered if I could be of some help to you."

Tom was surprised and hesitated a few moments.

Jerry misinterpreted Tom's hesitation. "Look, I don't want to butt in or anything. I just thought that maybe a little professional help—or even using me as a sounding board—might just be of some value."

"No," Tom said, "you're not butting in. I never have looked for a job before and, frankly, I do need some help."

"Great," said Jerry. "How about if I stop in after work and we'll talk about it?"

Later that afternoon, Jerry dropped by Tom's house, and they spent two hours working on his résumé. It didn't take Tom long to see how much help he really needed. Jerry took the résumé apart and put it back together, this time spelling out Tom's experience in broader terms. He highlighted his accomplishments and growth over the years. The concise, new résumé had more substance and clearly spelled out his objectives.

"Look," Jerry said, "why don't you let me take this with me? I can have it typed, and I'll get some copies run off."

Unknown to Tom, Jerry typed it himself and used the fine bond paper he had used for his own résumé. The next evening, Jerry delivered the final copies. Tom was pleased and impressed with the results. His offer to pay was waved away.

"Let's talk about personal contacts, target companies, and networking," Jerry suggested. "First, we should identify all of the companies that are competitive or similar to the one you left. Then we can get full information about them, including the names of the key executives, to develop a mailing list. You can find those in business libraries, but why don't you come over and spend a few hours at our office? I am sure I'll have some time to get you started."

"That sounds great!" exclaimed Tom.

Jerry smiled. "OK. Once we have the list of the companies that seem logical to approach, we will make up another list of all the people you know fairly well. Maybe they can help personally, but even if they can't, they may know others who might. These contacts may also know people in the very companies on our target list.

"This is the point of real networking. Every time you make a call, you want to get names. The more names we can get of people in our target companies, the better it is for us, because you can contact them in a more personalized way—namely, through your mutual friends."

They talked for another hour, going into further detail on how a contact base is established and expanded. By the end of the evening, Tom was stunned. He hardly knew this man, and yet he was getting more help—and professional help at that—than from anyone else he had known during his business career.

Within a week, Tom was well along on an active job search, and two weeks later, the first of several potential opportunities came his way. It was just about at this time, however, that John Grant, in response to his third customer complaint of the week, called the vice president of operations into his office.

"What's going on?" he demanded, after they reviewed the series of complaints.

"Well, John," the vice president replied, "we have a problem in coordinating our warehousing, inventory control, scheduling, and shipping. You remember I mentioned it a few months ago. I think we should bring in a topflight executive as superintendent over all of these functions."

John Grant turned slowly and looked out the window. After a few minutes, he turned back to the vice president of operations. "I do remember our conversation from a few months ago, and I made a mistake," he said. "We do need that sort of executive, and I know just the man."

It was an elated Tom Perrelli who called Jerry with the news. "It's a perfect job for me," he told him. "It's funny, but Mr. Grant apologized for not calling me sooner. Frankly, I think he added $5,000 to the salary because of the delay."

Jerry was delighted. He tried to minimize the help he had given Tom, but Tom wouldn't hear of it. "I really want to thank you, Jerry," Tom said. "I was at a low point, and to tell the truth, I'm still at a loss as to why you gave me so much help."

"Hey," Jerry laughed, "what are friends for?"

> "Which of these . . . do you think proved to be a neighbor to the man who fell into the robbers' hands?"

Obviously, those first "friends" Tom contacted were not friends in the sense that Jesus meant. Neither was Tom's pastor, who never even made a follow-up call to see how Tom was doing. John Grant's wife, Laura, was not a friend, and she let her social life take precedence over a person in need. In the end, John Grant might be considered a friend. After all, he had given Tom the job, but that was more for his own benefit.

Jerry Carson, on the other hand, was the real friend. When he saw a neighbor in need, he approached him with an offer to help. He didn't look for personal gain, and he wasn't motivated by greed or pride. He simply and selflessly gave what he had.

> And he said, "The one who showed mercy toward him." And Jesus said to him, "Go and do the same." (Luke 10:25-37)

When Tom Perrelli told me this story, he had been with his new company for about a year. He really enjoyed his new position, and both his responsibilities and his income had already been increased.

I had met Tom several years earlier because of the client relations I had with his prior company. At the time, I didn't get to know him too well because my work was not in his area, but I liked him and was pleased to hear how things had turned out after the company had been acquired.

I knew Jerry Carson a lot better, since he was my client contact during a number of assignments. His actions on Tom's behalf didn't surprise me at all.

In chapter 6 of the book of Micah in the Old Testament is found one of the greatest passages in the Bible—a summary of true religion. The prophet is asking what God expects of man and what will please him. In verse 6:8 it says:

> He has told you, O man, what is good; and what does
> the Lord require of you but to do justice, to love
> kindness, and to walk humbly with your God?

In all of my dealings with Jerry Carson, he impressed me as a person who followed those precepts. In the numerous meetings in which we participated, he was always kind and fair with everyone and exhibited not a shred of pomposity or boastfulness.

Jerry will probably never accumulate a lot of money. He is good at what he does, but he knows his limitations. His focus is not on higher-level positions or money as objectives in themselves. He earns an adequate income and leads a balanced life that includes quality time with his family and involvement in community and charitable activities. He and his wife lead a fairly simple but highly rewarding social life with a wide circle of friends.

He lives modestly and is putting money aside for his children's college educations. They in turn all work during the summer months to earn their spending money and are also saving for college. Jerry Carson is one of the most successful men I know. Over the years as our friendship grew, I had many serious discussions with him, and I am convinced that he has the perspective on success that we will now consider.

The Christian Perspective

Let's assume that after reading up to this point, a number of Christian men and women have identified with one or more of the particular points we've considered. Some now realize that the pursuit of money and the desire for material possessions have become so important in their lives that their relationship with God has become a secondary consideration. Others see that the cares of the world have done the same thing, and they have not been turning to God for help. In fact, they were even ignoring him.

Some have been able to see that they had let one or more of the "stumbling blocks" limit their progress, peace of mind, and happiness. Others have seen that they weren't using their talents effectively, and they were letting the laws and principles operative in this world work against them. A few have been lonely and had let love slip out of their lives, finding it difficult to maintain peace of mind and happiness. None have been honestly able to state that they were content with their lives.

Now let's make another assumption. By now, all of these readers have taken positive steps to overcome their particular problems. They have reordered their priorities and put God first in their lives, putting their trust in him. They are now making progress in using their talents more effectively. They are finding love returning to their lives, and for the first time, they have peace of mind knowing that they are saved. Since they are now using their talents more effectively, they are meeting or even exceeding their career goals. They are happier and more contented.

Is that it? Is that all there is? Or is there more?

The answer to the last question is yes—there is more—and I will outline why in this chapter. In fact, from a spiritual perspective, almost everything up to this point has been a prelude to what we will now consider.

First of all, we have a mighty God. He is greater than any perception we can have of him. His essence is love. It was because of his love that he sent his only begotten Son, Jesus Christ, as our Savior, and it is through him that we will find the "more" that is available to us.

To do that, we have to understand how Jesus looks at success and living successful lives. This is what we have been referring to as the Christian perspective.

The Prodigal Son

As we have seen, Jesus often told parables, or stories, that used analogies on the human level to make spiritual truths more easily understood. One of these, found in Luke 15, is referred to as the Parable of the Prodigal Son. The points Jesus made in this parable bear directly on the Christian perspective.

> "There was a man who had two sons. The younger one said to his father, 'Father, give me my share of the estate.' So he divided his property between them.
>
> "Not long after that, the younger son got together all he had, set off for a distant country and there squandered his wealth in wild living. After he had spent everything, there was a severe famine in that whole country, and he began to be in need. So

he went and hired himself out to a citizen of that country, who sent him to his fields to feed pigs. He longed to fill his stomach with the pods that the pigs were eating, but no one gave him anything.

"When he came to his senses, he said, 'How many of my father's hired men have food to spare, and here I am starving to death! I will set out and go back to my father and say to him: Father, I have sinned against heaven and against you. I am no longer worthy to be called your son; make me like one of your hired men.' So he got up and went to his father.

"But while he was still a long way off, his father saw him and was filled with compassion for him; he ran to his son, threw his arms around him and kissed him.

"The son said to him, 'Father, I have sinned against heaven and against you. I am no longer worthy to be called your son.'

"But the father said to his servants, 'Quick! Bring the best robe and put it on him. Put a ring on his finger and sandals on his feet. Bring the fattened calf and kill it. Let's have a feast and celebrate. For this son of mine was dead and is alive again; he was lost and is found.' So they began to celebrate."
(Luke 15:11-24, NIV)

Let's interrupt the story at this point. When he told this parable, Jesus chose his words very carefully. He was sitting with tax collectors and sinners who could identify with the younger son. Many of them were living lifestyles that alienated them from God, and they were excluded from the religious community. Also listening to Jesus were Pharisees (members of a strict Jewish sect) and scribes (professional interpreters of the Law).

The sins Jesus attributed to the son were extremely serious in the Pharisees' and scribes' eyes. Not only had the son lived a wild life with harlots, but he had also broken custom by asking for his share of his father's estate. Particularly repugnant to the Pharisees and scribes was his job feeding pigs. They would have absolutely nothing to do with swine, and they considered anyone who did to be ceremonially unclean.

Yet here was Jesus describing the father running to meet his son, embracing and kissing him. He didn't wait for a litany of his sins. Instead, he quickly got him a fine robe, a large ring, and new sandals. To show his joy at his son's return, he ordered his servants to prepare a celebration feast.

What this part of the parable shows is that for a period of time, the son had broken fellowship with his father, but he had not lost his position in the family. He was still his father's son, and upon his return, he was welcomed back with joy.

When we sin, we also break fellowship with God, but we do not lose our position in his family. We are still sons and daughters of the Father, and he is waiting for us to return. Because of his unconditional love, he will "run" to meet us with compassion and joy.

It should be noted that Jesus did not name his parables. In this case, he simply started talking about a man who had two sons. Because most Christians refer to it as the Parable of the Prodigal Son, however, the significance of the last part, which concerns the older brother, is often overlooked. Jesus didn't tell stories idly. He was making two points in this parable, and they are equally important. Now let's return to the parable, the part where the celebration has begun.

> "Meanwhile, the older son was in the field. When he came near the house, he heard music and dancing. So he called one of the servants and asked him what was going on. 'Your brother has come,' he replied, 'and your father has killed the fattened calf because he has him back safe and sound.'

"The older brother became angry and refused to go in. So his father went out and pleaded with him. But he answered his father, 'Look! All these years I've been slaving for you and never disobeyed your orders. Yet you never gave me even a young goat so I could celebrate with my friends. But when this son of yours who has squandered your property with prostitutes comes home, you kill the fattened calf for him!'

" 'My son,' the father said, 'you are always with me, and everything I have is yours. But we had to celebrate and be glad, because this brother of yours was dead and is alive again; he was lost and is found.' " (Luke 15:25-32, NIV)

Obviously, the older son did not understand his relationship with his father. He had not been taking advantage of what was available to him and what was rightfully his.

Unfortunately, many Christians (quite possibly the majority of us) are living our lives in a similar manner. If so, then the true fruits of success will continue to elude us, and we will never flourish to our full potential.

Look at the words of the older son. First, he said he had been "slaving" for his father while his brother was gone. Although he had been living in the midst of his father's abundance—where everything his father had was his—he had not appropriated any of it. Instead, what he had done was to compartmentalize his life, relying on himself as he worked and ignoring his father in the process. How many of us have done the same thing in our lives?

Then the son stated that he had "never disobeyed." Apparently this was his idea of how to please his father—he hadn't disobeyed him.

Many Christians see their relationship with God in the same way. They make "sin avoidance" a major focus of their lives. What they are really doing is setting up a false standard that they can never meet. When they do sin, feelings of guilt and unworthiness can easily develop.

In Matthew 22:35-40, a lawyer asked Jesus what was the greatest commandment. Jesus replied: "'You shall love the Lord your God with all your heart, and with all your soul, and with all your mind.' This is the great and foremost commandment. The second is like it, 'You shall love your neighbor as yourself.' On these two commandments depend the whole Law and the Prophets."

Jesus put all the commandments into two great positives—love of God and love of neighbor. It is a loving heart that God seeks, and when we follow those two commandments, "sin avoidance" becomes the result rather than the focus.

Finally, the older son complained that his father had never given him a feast so that he could celebrate with his friends. Again, we see the compartmentalizing. The son did not view the feast in terms of intimacy and joy with his father. Rather, he saw the feast as a way to have fun with his friends. It's also apparent that he never asked his father for a feast. We know everything the father had was his, but the son had focused so much on "self" that he had never developed a close relationship with his father—a relationship that would have made every meal a time of joy and celebration.

The older brother's reaction is similar to the way many Christians think. When they see others who seem happier and more blessed by God, they are filled with envy, resentment, and self-pity. The fact that they have compartmentalized their lives and not cultivated a relationship with God hasn't occurred to them.

In the second half of the Parable of the Prodigal Son, Jesus is trying to help us understand what our relationship is supposed to be like with God the Father. We are his children, and the parable makes it clear that everything he has is ours. The way we enjoy that relationship is through our personal relationship with Jesus Christ, which is established the moment we accept him as Lord and Savior of our lives.

The Vine and Branches

In the fifteenth chapter of the Gospel of John, Jesus gives an analogy to show the nature of our relationship with him. The chapter starts with Jesus likening himself to a vine. The Father is the vinedresser, and we are the branches.

As part of the vine, we are intimately linked with Jesus, where our spiritual life is his spiritual life. In verses 4 and 5, he states this clearly:

> "Abide in Me, and I in you. As the branch cannot bear fruit of itself, unless it abides in the vine, so neither can you, unless you abide in Me. I am the vine, you are the branches; he who abides in Me, and I in him, he bears much fruit; for apart from Me you can do nothing."

When we look at a vine, it's obvious that if a branch is lying on the ground, it will wither and die. In order to have life, it must be part of the vine. The way we know that the branch is receiving its life from the vine is when it produces fruit. In other words, the fruit is the evidence that the life of the vine is flowing into the branch. When Jesus says we abide in him, there should also be evidence that his spiritual life is flowing into us.

What are the fruits that should be evident in our lives? The answer is found in Paul's letter to the Ephesians. Paul says:

> For we are His workmanship, created in Christ Jesus for good works, which God prepared beforehand, that we should walk in them. (Ephesians 2:10)

Good works. These are the fruits that should be the evidence of our relationship with Jesus. But we are not saved by those good works, as Paul clearly states in verses 8 and 9 of that same chapter:

> For by grace you have been saved through faith; and that not of yourselves, it is the gift of God; not as a result of works, that no one should boast.

We are saved by grace, but we are called to do good works. Grace has been defined as the "unmerited favor of God." It comes to us because of his love and is filled with his compassion, mercy, and power. It is because of grace that we have been grafted on to the vine, where the life of Jesus can flow into us, clearing the way for us to do good works. It should be noted that these works were planned for us by God beforehand, so when we perform them, we are walking in his will and according to his plan.

But let's reflect further for a moment. Even though we are attached to the vine, of ourselves we cannot do the good works planned for us. The branch can only produce fruit because of the life and power that flows through it from the vine.

Can you see how reliant we are on Jesus to live the way he wants us to live? God has a plan for each of us, and he has prepared good works for us to do. Because of the spiritual life flowing to us from Jesus, we can be fruitful. As opportunities for good works appear, our minds are open to see them. Then the grace flowing through us from Jesus empowers us to do them.

Our role is to cooperate with the grace being given to us. We have been chosen by God to be the means by which he carries out his plans. Our ability to actually perform good works stems from the talents he has given us. For example, if a particular good work is providing financial help for someone in need, then it was God who blessed us with the talent to earn enough money to provide that help.

In most instances, however, doing good works doesn't relate to money at all. We can offer a kind word of encourage-ment or go to someone in need and help solve their problems. We can touch people with love because we have the love of Je-sus flowing through us. We can be friends to the lonely, we can comfort the sorrowful, and we can visit the sick.

The list goes on and on. While the opportunities for good works are endless, this doesn't mean we have to go out looking for them. God has planned the opportunities for good works, and he will open our eyes to see them. In the meantime, we want to live his way, trusting and relying on him while cooper-ating when his Spirit directs us.

Many people have a tendency to think of good works in terms of major events, but that is not always the case.

One Sunday after a Bible study class, a young mother talked with me about this subject of good works. We stood in the hall-way and chatted while her husband was picking up their three children from their Sunday school classes.

The gist of her conversation was that she regretted not hav-ing the time or opportunity to do many good works. Her days were filled with caring for the children and carrying out an al-most infinite number of chores around the house. I was struck by the irony of her words.

Here was a loving wife and mother who handled all the re-sponsibilities put in front of her. She nurtured her children and taught them to love the Lord. She was a wife, a cook, a nurse, a teacher, a purchasing agent, a chauffeur, and a housekeeper. Her life as a stay-at-home mom was actually overflowing in good works every day. She was walking in God's will for this period of her life. After the children are grown, he may have other plans for her, and if so, he will let her know.

As I outlined all the good works she was doing during this season of motherhood, this mom suddenly saw the reality of her life. Her eyes filled with tears, and she embraced me with a sis-terly hug. Then we prayed together for a few moments. She thanked God for her new understanding, and I thanked him for the opportunity he had just given me.

Real Peace

It should be clear now why we want to cultivate a personal relationship with Jesus. In those verses about the vine in John 15, Jesus tells us that when we produce fruit, the Father prunes the branches so that we can produce even more fruit. The Holy Spirit is continually molding and shaping us, bringing us closer to the likeness of Jesus. As he does, our lives become more fruitful.

Earlier, I pointed out that the promises of God are always conditional, and when we read John 15, we see that the condition for us to produce fruit is to abide in Jesus and have him abide in us. How do we do that? In verse 10, Jesus shows us the way: "If you keep My commandments, you will abide in My love; just as I have kept My Father's commandments, and abide in His love."

Well, we already know his commandments: Love God and love your neighbor. If we obey these two, we are abiding in him. As we cultivate our relationship with Jesus, making it deeper and more intimate, we are increasingly aware of his love, and his spiritual life flows into us more fully, enhancing our ability to love and to produce fruit. In this relationship, we can see the true nature of the fruits of success.

Peace of mind initially comes to us when we are saved, but the fruit of success can flourish still more fully. The peace of mind we want goes beyond the sureness of salvation. In John 14:27, Jesus describes the ultimate peace that can be ours here on earth: "Peace I leave with you; My peace I give to you; not as the world gives, do I give to you. Let not your heart be troubled, nor let it be fearful."

This is the true fruit of peace—the peace of Jesus Christ. It can soothe our hearts and overcome our fears. It is not the limited form of peace the world experiences from time to time, nor is it tied to financial security. Rather, we can have the unlimited peace of Jesus himself.

The extent of that peace is shown in Paul's letter to the Philippians: "Be anxious for nothing, but in everything by prayer and supplication with thanksgiving let your requests be made known to God. And the peace of God, which surpasses all comprehension, shall guard your hearts and your minds in Christ Jesus" (Philippians 4:6-7).

This, then, is the true fruit of peace. It is the peace of God that surpasses all comprehension, and it comes to us through our relationship with Jesus Christ.

Nothing Too Large or Too Difficult

From time to time, we all run into situations that lead to anxieties. When these "stumbling blocks" appear, we can immediately turn to Jesus for help. If we put our trust in Christ, no problems are too large or too difficult for him. His peace will become our peace, allowing us to deal with the problem calmly and objectively.

Now let's consider happiness. When we looked at it from a material perspective, we saw that it flows from personal relationships. As Christians, however, we are not limited to the human level. We have the advantage of a personal relationship with Jesus—a relationship that transcends all others. In that same chapter about the vine, John 15, Jesus tells us, "These things I have spoken to you, that My joy may be in you, and that your joy may be made full" (John 15:11).

In this verse, Jesus elevates happiness to joy, and the true fruit of happiness is the joy of Jesus himself—a joy that will fill us completely. When we are abiding in Jesus and his spiritual life is flowing freely to us, we can be fruitful. In this intimate relationship, our happiness is elevated to the joy of Jesus.

Contentment should now be easy to understand. True contentment comes not from what we do, but from what Jesus does through us. If we think in terms of ourselves, we will always have regrets over the number of times we have fallen or the goals we didn't achieve. As our relationship with Jesus deepens, however, we will come to the realization that it is his life and his power that enable us to do anything good. Our cooperation with grace allows him to live his life through us, and in this way we can taste the true fruit of contentment.

Knowing that the fruits of success come to us through our personal relationship with Jesus raises an important question. Since that relationship with him is established the moment we accept him as Savior, why do so many Christians still find the fruits of success so elusive? The answer lies in understanding the importance of cultivating our relationship with Christ.

Before we knew Jesus, our entire focus was on "self." And why not? But since that self-focus was so ingrained in us when we accepted God's gift of salvation, the relationship that was established could be called "Me and Jesus." Unfortunately, that's where many Christians leave it. If we do that—keeping "self" in the forefront and Jesus in second place—we will never be able to live the fruitful life God has planned for us. The true fruits of success will continue to elude us.

Please understand that we are not talking about salvation here. We have already accepted God's gift, and it is ours. What we are talking about is living successfully, taking advantage of the grace that is offered to us each day, and having the fruits of success flourish in our lives to their full potential. This is the real meaning of success, and it can only happen by deepening our relationship with Jesus and making it more intimate.

To accomplish that, consider how we develop personal relationships with other people. The first step is an introduction. As we spend time with them, we get to know each other better. Then we look for opportunities to share experiences and to learn what they think about various subjects and events. We want to become friends, and we desire to please them. For genuine friendship to develop, they also must have an interest in us.

The steps outlined above are the same for deepening a relationship with Jesus, although we have some built-in advantages to start with. We have already met him, and a personal relationship has begun. He graciously makes himself available to us all the time. He already knows all about us and, in spite of our faults and weaknesses, he loves us unconditionally. We know he is interested in everything we do.

In the section of John's Gospel where Jesus likens himself to a vine, we read in 15:5 that in order to bear fruit, we must abide in Jesus. Then in verse 7, Jesus states: "If you abide in Me, and My words abide in you, ask whatever you wish, and it shall be done for you."

In that verse, Jesus tell us clearly how to deepen a relationship with him. Abide means to "reside" or "continue to stay." Since we are the branches and his life is flowing in us, we already are abiding in him. But then he added that his words should also abide in us. His words are found in the Bible, and all we have to do to know them is to read them.

Reading Scripture is the single best way to cultivate our personal relationship with Jesus. We cannot overemphasize the importance of this. As we read, the words go first into our minds, and then settle into our hearts. We get to know more about him, what he has done for us, and what he continues to do. The Holy Spirit enlightens our minds, and the words become alive. The more we read, the more we understand and the deeper our relationship grows. When the words of Jesus are in our hearts, they are abiding in us.

The Bible is also clear that because of our relationship with Jesus, we can enter into the house of the Father, where everything he has is ours. We've already seen evidence of that when we considered Paul's letter to the Philippians. In chapter 4:6-7, we are told to be anxious for nothing but to let our prayer requests be known. We see that same ability to go directly to the Father many times in Scripture. In the letter to the Hebrews, we are told: "Let us therefore draw near with confidence to the throne of grace, that we may receive mercy and may find grace to help in time of need" (Hebrews 4:16).

We can only have the fruits of success flourishing steadily in our lives by being filled with the grace of God. In order to do that, the spiritual life of Jesus has to flow freely to us. If we keep our focus on "self," we are restricting that flow. The "Me and Jesus" relationship has to change.

Let me illustrate this by a story.

Suppose a man is traveling through a jungle with a guide. The trail is obscured by overgrown vines. The man uses a machete to clear a path, but then the guide—who knows the jungle paths like the back of his hand—offers to lead. He also has a much larger machete.

The man says, "Thanks, but I think I can handle this" to the offer, and he still continues to lead. Progress is slow as he fights to clear away the vines and stay on the trail. As the man sweats and strains, the guide walks effortlessly behind him. On some occasions, the man can't even see the path, and he becomes completely entangled in the vines. When he calls out for help, the guide quickly disentangles him. Soon, they are traveling back in the right direction.

As they work their way through the jungle, the man talks with the guide and gets to know him better. Finally, it dawns on him that he has not chosen the best way to get to his destination, so he asks the guide to take the lead. The guide hacks through the vines easily, and progress is more rapid. The man learns quickly, however, that he must crouch lower, or the higher vines will snap into his face. He crouches lower and the trip becomes smoother and easier.

If we convert this parable to our relationship with Jesus, we should realize that it is both inappropriate and ineffectual to go through life with the King of kings walking behind us. In the Bible, Jesus describes himself as the Light of the world. We want that light out in front of us where we can see ahead, rather than having it behind us. He also said that he is the Truth and the Way. Again, we want the truth in front of us where we can see it and walk in it. We also want the Person who knows the way to guide us.

When we have our relationship as "Me and Jesus," we are still relying on ourselves to wrestle with the cares of the world. But if the words of Jesus sink into our hearts, we will realize that we want to follow him rather than trying to lead. When we make that decision, our relationship changes to "Jesus and Me."

When this happens—when the words of Jesus are abiding in our hearts and Jesus is first in our relationship—we have found the true fruits of success, clearing the path to live successful lives.

We must realize, however, that there are degrees of peace, happiness, and contentment. They will flourish more freely when the "Me" in the relationship is reduced and changes to the lowercased version: "me." As we experience the true fruits of success, we will want to reduce our self-focus as much as possible. This will happen if we continue deepening our relationship with Jesus, looking for ways to make it more intimate. The decision is up to us.

We took a major step when we let Jesus move into ascendancy and be first in our lives. We realized that of ourselves we cannot lead successful lives, but that he can. If we want the fruits of success to flourish to the fullness of their potential, we must continue to reduce self-focus and let Jesus live his life through us.

When we look at good works objectively, we become aware that our role should not be a source of personal pride. God planned them and set up all the circumstances. He endowed us with the talents that permit us to help others. When we do good works, we are being used by God. We are walking in his will, and the joy we feel is the joy of Jesus. We can only thank him and give him all the glory. When we do that, we are truly "storing up treasures in heaven."

We live in an imperfect world where we ourselves are imperfect. Accordingly, that self-focus will reappear from time to time, and it's inevitable that we will sin on occasion. Sometimes the cares of the world can crowd in on us, or we will encounter major adversities. All of these situations can cause us to lose the fruits of success temporarily. But if the words of Jesus are abiding in us, we will quickly turn back to him. Our relationship will be restored, and we will find strength and healing that will let them flourish anew.

The Final Step

There is one final step in our relationship with Jesus, but it will not occur here on earth. That final step will come when we meet him face-to-face. When we finally see him in all of his majesty and shining glory, we will experience the fullness and depth of his love for us.

When that happens, we will not lose our personal identity. In fact, I believe our identity will actually be heightened. As the love of Christ envelops us, we will bow before him, and the fruits of success will blossom beyond anything that we can now conceive. The final relationship will then simply be:

JESUS.

Conclusion

A few months ago I was out of town on business and was finishing a quiet dinner in the hotel dining room. I happened to glance at a nearby table where three men and a woman were already eating their desserts.

Because of the centerpiece on their table and the way they were sitting, I couldn't see what they were having, but it was obvious from the expression on the woman's face that she was very happy with whatever she had chosen. The men who were dining with her seemed less satisfied. They were picking at their desserts and were showing little, if any, pleasure in them.

I asked my waiter what dessert the woman was having, telling him that I didn't want what the men at the table had selected. He looked at me and seemed perplexed. He told me their dessert orders were all the same.

It occurred to me later that this group of people is analogous to Christians in general. While many are finding joy in their Christianity, there appears to be an even greater number who are not. They are very much like the older brother in the Parable of the Prodigal Son, "slaving" away as they try to follow the rules and regulations that have been ingrained in them as being essential ingredients of their religion. But what are these rules and regulations?

All too often they are man-made and are judgmental and legalistic in nature. They establish false standards that limit the intimacy of our relationship with Jesus. They are not based on biblical truths, and they can never substitute for the grace we need each day to lead our lives the way God intends for us to lead them. Little wonder that people who try to follow them find their Christianity a somber and unsatisfying experience. Like the older brother, they are not enjoying the "feast" their Father has prepared for them.

Legalisms are forms of bondages and, like all bondages, they blur the reality of God. Jesus is not legalistic, and he came to free us from bondages, not to impose them on us. Our relationship with him need not be complicated. If we make it simpler, less intellectual, less philosophical, and free of legalisms, we will know the reality of God, and our relationship with him will be far more meaningful and rewarding.

One of my objectives in writing this book was to show the nature of the true fruits of success—peace of mind, happiness, and contentment—and how we can have them flourish in our lives through our personal relationship with Jesus.

Writing it, however, has taken a lot longer than I had anticipated at the outset. At that time I felt strongly God wanted me to write it, and the format of what I was to cover seemed quite clear. In doing it, however, I ran into problems.

One was concerned with time. Basically, I had only the weekends to write, and there were often distractions that interfered with my progress. Further, while I was able to handle the practical aspects of the book quite readily, I kept getting tied up in problems when it came to the spiritual aspects.

I kept at it, however, and finally the book was completed. Then came the disappointment. As I read and reread the finished product, I knew it wasn't right. I also knew that Jesus wasn't satisfied with it.

In my discouragement I put the book aside for many

months. Yet, the nagging feeling that God still wanted me to do it remained. I fought that feeling for a while, but I finally surrendered. I did then what I should have been doing all along. I turned to Jesus for help.

I spent more time reading the Bible, meditating on it, and asking God for guidance. Gradually the answers to my problems became clear. He had given me the idea of what he wanted, but then I had gone off, relying on my own resources to carry it out. The story that we used earlier of the man traveling through a jungle along an obscure path is a perfect illustration of what I had been doing. A Guide had offered to show me the way, but I had been keeping him behind me. It became clear to me that Jesus had to be first, and with that knowledge, I began rewriting the manuscript.

Before each writing period I renewed my mind by reading the Bible. I asked the Holy Spirit to enlighten my mind, and I asked Jesus to lead the way.

Instead of striving and struggling, the words and thoughts began to flow more easily. From time to time I would still go off on tangents, but I had become more sensitive to his direction and would quickly come back and follow him again. When it came to the chapter on the Christian perspective, it was almost like taking dictation. As I look back, I realize now that there was no possible way that I could have written that chapter when I first started. Nor could I have done it this time, unless he had guided me through it step by step.

In that chapter, Jesus shows the nature of the true fruits of success and exactly how we can make them ours. He is with us to help us, and he wants us to rely on him every moment of our lives. He wants us to find the joy that is intended for us in our relationship with him, and because of his love and grace, he enables us to have it regardless of our circumstances.

As I read the Bible, I could see that there were many other parables and verses of Scripture that I could have used to reach the same conclusions that are made in this book. Whenever I tried to include any of them, however, it didn't work. He wanted me to use the ones that he told me to use, and he made it clear that if I was to follow his plan, I had to do it his way.

I don't know exactly how God intends to use this book. I hope, of course, that it is to help other Christians find the true fruits of success, and that in doing so, they find joy in their Christianity.

There is another major reason for Christians to find that joy, and it goes beyond just the benefits of leading a satisfying life. The greatest good work that any of us can perform is to help lead another person to Jesus. While few of us are called to be missionaries, evangelists, pastors, or clergymen, we are all called to be witnesses. The best way we can do that is to let our lives be a witness for us.

If we are unhappy or unsatisfied with the Christian life we are leading, why would anyone else want to have what we have? Think of it. The reason I wanted the dessert the woman had ordered at the hotel was because she was so obviously enjoying it.

This illustrates the other reason why we should be joyous in our Christianity. We are not going to help people know and accept Jesus by arguing or debating with them. Trying to look pious and holy won't work very well either. But if we are finding great happiness and joy in our relationship with him, his love will be shining right through us for others to see.

People who don't know Jesus are living with a void inside their hearts—a void that cannot be filled with money or worldly pleasures. If they sense that what we have can fill that void—if they want what we have—some of them are going to try to find out what it is. If their eyes are opened and they accept Jesus as their Savior, the joy we will experience in their salvation will truly be his joy.

As Christians, we already know and have a personal relationship with Jesus, and there is nothing more precious in this world. Our relationship with him is intended to be happy and joyous. But we also know that the Christian life is not trouble free, and problems will come our way. We will have our down times. We will get angry, say things that we will regret, and we will make mistakes. He is always with us, however, and when we ask for his forgiveness and help, we will receive it. In our daily walk with him, we want to heed the advice that Paul gives us in Philippians 4:4:

"Rejoice in the Lord always; again I will say, rejoice!"

About the Author

Frank R. Beaudine is chairman and CEO of Eastman & Beaudine, Inc., a major international executive recruiting firm. In an industry with more than four thousand competitors, his company is recognized as one of the top fifty recruiting firms in the country.

After graduating from the University of Notre Dame with a degree in chemical engineering, he spent three years on active duty as a Naval officer aboard a destroyer. His early business career was with several well-known firms, including Uniroyal and Montgomery Ward. After several years as a general consultant with the prestigious firm of McKinsey & Company, he served for five years as vice president of operations for a division of Norton Simon, Inc. He joined Eastman & Beaudine when it was formed in 1967, becoming president in 1971, CEO in 1974, and chairman in 1978.

A prolific writer, he has had numerous articles published over the years in major business magazines and newspapers, such as the *Wall Street Journal*. He served several years on the board of directors of the recruiting industries professional organization and is currently on the advisory boards of the Salvation Army and the Josh McDowell Ministry.

Mr. Beaudine and his wife, Martha, are the parents of four grown children and have nine grandchildren. They reside in a suburb of Dallas.